MY LITERARY PASSIONS

BY

W. D. HOWELLS

GREENWOOD PRESS, PUBLISHERS
NEW YORK

Originally published in 1895
by Harper and Brothers Publishers

First Greenwood Reprinting, 1969

Library of Congress Catalogue Card Number 68-57612

PRINTED IN UNITED STATES OF AMERICA

MY LITERARY PASSIONS.

—◆—

I.

THE BOOKCASE AT HOME.

To give an account of one's reading is in some sort to give an account of one's life; and I hope that I shall not offend those who follow me in these papers, if I cannot help speaking of myself in speaking of the authors I must call my masters: my masters not because they taught me this or that directly, but because I had such delight in them that I could not fail to teach myself from them whatever I was capable of learning. I do not know whether I have been what people call a great reader; I cannot claim even to have been a very wise reader; but I have always been conscious of a high purpose to read much more, and more discreetly, than I have ever really done, and probably it is from the vantage-ground of this good intention that I shall sometimes be found writing here rather than from the facts of the case.

But I am pretty sure that I began right, and that if I had always kept the lofty level which I struck at the outset I should have the right to use authority in these reminiscences without a bad conscience. I shall try not to use authority, however, and I do not expect to speak here of all my reading, whether it has been much or little, but only of those books, or of those authors that I have felt a genuine passion for. I have known such passions at every period of my life, but it is mainly of the loves of my youth that I shall write, and I shall write all the more frankly because my own youth now seems to me rather more alien than that of any other person.

I think that I came of a reading race, which has always loved literature in a way, and in spite of varying fortunes and many changes. From a letter of my great-grandmother's written to a stubborn daughter upon some unfilial behavior, like running away to be married, I suspect that she was fond of the high-colored fiction of her day, for she tells the willful child that she has " planted a dagger in her mother's heart," and I should not be surprised if it were from this fine-languaged lady that my grandfather derived his taste for poetry, rather than from his father, who was of a worldly-wiser mind. To be sure, he became a Friend by Convincement, as the Quakers say, and so I cannot imagine that he was altogether worldly; but he had an eye to the main chance: he founded the industry of making flannels in the little Welsh town where he lived, and he seems to have grown richer, for his day and place, than any of us have since grown for ours. My grandfather, indeed, was concerned chiefly in getting away from the world and its wickedness. He came to this country early in the century and settled his family in a log-cabin in the Ohio woods, that they might be safe from the sinister influences of the village where he was managing some woolen mills. But he kept his affection for certain poets of the graver, not to say gloomier sort, and he must have suffered his children to read them, pending that great question of their souls' salvation which was a lifelong trouble to him.

My father, at any rate, had such a decided bent in the direction of literature, that he was not content in any of his several economical experiments till he became the editor of a newspaper, which was then the sole means of satisfying a literary passion. His paper, at the date when I began to know him, was a living, comfortable and decent, but without the least promise of wealth in it, or the hope even of a much better condition. I think now that he was wise not to care for the advancement which most of us have our hearts set upon, and that it was one of his finest qualities that he was content with a lot in life where he was not exempt from work with his hands, and yet where he was not so pressed by need but he could give himself at will not only to the things of the spirit, but the things of the mind too. After a season of skepticism he had become a religious man, like the rest of his race, but in his own fashion, which was not at all the fashion of my grandfather: a Friend who had married out of Meeting, and had ended a perfervid Methodist. My father, who could never get himself converted at any of the camp-meetings where my grandfather often led the forces of prayer to his support, and had at last to be given up in despair, fell in with the writings of Emanuel Swedenborg, and embraced the doctrine of that philosopher with a content that has lasted him all the days of his many years. Ever since I can remember, the works of Swedenborg formed a large part of his library; he read them much himself, and much to my mother, and occasionally a "Memorable Relation" from them to us children. But he did not force them upon our notice, nor urge us to read them, and I think this was very well. I suppose his conscience and his reason kept him from doing so. But in regard to other books, his fondness was too much for him, and when I began to show a liking for literature he was eager to guide my choice.

His own choice was for poetry, and the most of our library, which was not given to theology, was given to poetry. I call it the library now, but then we called it the bookcase, and that was what literally it was, though I believe that whatever we had called our modest collection of books, it was a larger private collection than any other in the town where we lived. Still it was all held, and shut with glass doors, in a case of very few shelves. It was not considerably enlarged during my childhood, for few books came to my father as editor, and he indulged himself in buying them even more rarely. My grandfather's bookstore (it was also the village drug-store) had then the only stock of literature for sale in the place; and once, when Harper & Brothers' agent came to replenish it, he gave my father several volumes for review. One of these was a copy of Thomson's Seasons, a finely-illustrated edition, whose pictures I knew long before I knew the poetry, and thought them the most beautiful things that ever were. My father read passages of the book aloud, and he wanted me to read it

all myself. For the matter of that he wanted me to
read Cowper, from whom no one could get anything
but good, and he wanted me to read Byron, from
whom I could then have got no harm; we get harm
from the evil we understand. He loved Burns, too,
and he used to read aloud from him, I must own, to
my inexpressible weariness. I could not away with
that dialect, and I could not then feel the charm of
the poet's wit, nor the tender beauty of his pathos.
Moore, I could manage better; and when my father
read Lalla Rookh to my mother I sat up to listen, and
entered into all the woes of Iran in the story of the
Fire Worshippers. I drew the line at the Veiled
Prophet of Khorassan, though I had some sense of the
humor of the poet's conception of the critic in Fadla-
deen. But I liked Scott's poems far better, and got
from Ispahan to Edinburgh with a glad alacrity of
fancy. I followed the Lady of the Lake throughout,
and when I first b ran to contrive verses of my own I
found that poem a fit model in mood and metre.

Among other volumes of verse on the top shelf of the
bookcase, of which I used to look at the outside without penetrating deeply within, were Pope's translation
of the Iliad and the Odyssey, and Dryden's Virgil,
pretty little tomes in tree-calf, published by James

Crissy in Philadelphia, and illustrated with small copper-plates, which somehow seemed to put the matter hopelessly beyond me. It was as if they said to me in so many words that literature which furnished the subjects of such pictures I could not hope to understand, and need not try. At any rate, I let them alone for the time, and I did not meddle with a volume of Shakespeare, in green cloth and cruelly fine print, which overawed me in like manner with its wood-cuts. I cannot say just why I conceived that there was something unhallowed in the matter of the book; perhaps this was a tint from the reputation of the rather profligate young man from whom my father had it. If he were not profligate I ask his pardon. I have not the least notion who he was, but that was the notion I had of him, whoever he was, or wherever he now is. There may never have been such a young man at all; the impression I had may have been pure invention of my own, after the manner of children who do not very distinctly know their dreams from their experiences, and live in the world where both project the same quality of shadow.

There were, of course, other books in the bookcase, which my consciousness made no account of, and I speak only of those I remember. Fiction there was

none at all that I can recall, except Poe's Tales of the
Grotesque and the Arabesque (I long afflicted myself
as to what those words meant, when I might easily
have asked and found out) and Bulwer's Last Days of
Pompeii, all in the same kind of binding. History is
known, to my young remembrance of that library, by
a History of the United States, whose dust and ashes
I hardily made my way through; and by a Chronicle
of the Conquest of Granada, by the ever dear and
precious Fray Antonio Agapida, whom I was long in
making out to be one and the same as Washington
Irving.

In school there was as little literature then as there
is now, and I cannot say anything worse of our school
reading; but I was not really very much in school,
and so I got small harm from it. The printing-office
was my school from a very early date. My father
thoroughly believed in it, and he had his beliefs as to
work, which he illustrated as soon as we were old
enough to learn the trade he followed. We could go
to school and study, or we could go into the printing-
office and work, with an equal chance of learning, but
we could not be idle; we must do something, for our
souls' sake, though he was willing enough we should
play, and he liked himself to go into the woods with

us, and to enjoy the pleasures that manhood can share with childhood. I suppose that as the world goes now we were poor. His income was never above twelve hundred a year, and his family was large ; but nobody was rich there or then; we lived in the simple abundance of that time and place, and we did not know that we were poor. As yet the unequal modern conditions were undreamed of (who indeed could have dreamed of them forty or fifty years ago?) in the little Southern Ohio town where nearly the whole of my most happy boyhood was passed.

II.

GOLDSMITH.

When I began to have literary likings of my own, and to love certain books above others, the first authors of my heart were Goldsmith, Cervantes, and Irving. In the sharply foreshortened perspective of the past I seem to have read them all at once, but I am aware of an order of time in the pleasure they gave me, and I know that Goldsmith came first. He came so early that I cannot tell when or how I began to read him, but it must have been before I was ten years old. I read other books about that time, notably a small book on Grecian and Roman mythology, which I perused with such a passion for those pagan gods and goddesses that, if it had ever been a question of sacrificing to Diana, I do not really know whether I should have been able to refuse. I adored indiscriminately all the tribes of nymphs and naiads, demigods and heroes, as well as the high ones of

Olympus; and I am afraid that by day I dwelt in a
world peopled and ruled by them, though I faithfully
said my prayers at night, and fell asleep in sorrow for
my sins. I do not know in the least how Goldsmith's
Greece came into my hands, though I fancy it must
have been procured for me because of a taste which
I showed for that kind of reading, and I can imagine
no greater luck for a small boy in a small town of
Southwestern Ohio well-nigh fifty years ago. I have
the books yet; two little, stout volumes in fine print,
with the marks of wear on them, but without those
dishonorable blots, or those other injuries which boys
inflict upon books in resentment of their dullness, or
out of mere wantonness. I was always sensitive to
the maltreatment of books; I could not bear to see a
book faced down or dogs-eared or broken-backed. It
was like a hurt or an insult to a thing that could feel.

Goldsmith's history of Rome came to me much
later, but quite as immemorably, and after I had
formed a preference for the Greek Republics, which I
dare say was not mistaken. Of course I liked Athens
best, and yet there was something in the fine behavior
of the Spartans in battle, which won a heart formed
for hero-worship. I mastered the notion of their
communism, and approved of their iron money, with

the poverty it obliged them to, yet somehow their
cruel treatment of the Helots failed to shock me;
perhaps I forgave it to their patriotism, as I had to
forgive many ugly facts in the history of the Romans
to theirs.   There was hardly any sort of bloodshed
which I would not pardon in those days to the
slayers of tyrants; and the swagger form of such as
dispatched a despot with a fine speech was so much
to my liking that I could only grieve that I was born
too late to do and to say those things.

I do not think I yet felt the beauty of the literature
which made them all live in my fancy, that I conceived of Goldsmith as an artist using for my rapture
the finest of the arts; and yet I had been taught to
see the loveliness of poetry, and was already trying to
make it on my own poor account.   I tried to make
verses like those I listened to when my father read
Moore and Scott to my mother, but I heard them
with no such happiness as I read my beloved histories,
though I never thought then of attempting to write
like Goldsmith.   I accepted his beautiful work as ignorantly as I did my other blessings.   I was concerned
in getting at the Greeks and Romans, and I did not
know through what nimble air and by what lovely
ways I was led to them.   Some retrospective percep-

tion of this came long afterward when I read his essays, and after I knew all of his poetry, and later yet when I read the Vicar of Wakefield; but for the present my eyes were holden, as the eyes of a boy mostly are in the world of art. What I wanted with my Greeks and Romans after I got at them was to be like them, or at least to turn them to account in verse, and in dramatic verse at that. The Romans were less civilized than the Greeks, and so were more like boys, and more to a boy's purpose. I did not make literature of the Greeks, but I got a whole tragedy out of the Romans; it was a rhymed tragedy, and in octosyllabic verse, like the Lady of the Lake. I meant it to be acted by my schoolmates, but I am not sure that I ever made it known to them. Still, they were not ignorant of my reading, and I remember how proud I was when a certain boy, who had always whipped me when we fought together, and so outranked me in that little boys' world, once sent to ask me the name of the Roman emperor who lamented at nightfall, when he had done nothing worthy, that he had lost a day. The boy was going to use the story in a composition, as we called the school themes then, and I told him the emperor's name; I could not tell him now without turning to the book.

My reading gave me no standing among the boys, and I did not expect it to rank me with boys who were more valiant in fight or in play ; and I have since found that literature gives one no more certain station in the world of men's activities, either idle or useful. We literary folk try to believe that it does, but that is all nonsense. At every period of life, among boys or men, we are accepted when they are at leisure, and want to be amused, and at best we are tolerated rather than accepted. I must have told the boys stories out of my Goldsmith's Greece and Rome or it would not have been known that I had read them, but I have no recollection now of doing so, while I distinctly remember rehearsing the allegories and fables of the Gesta Romanorum, a book which seems to have been in my hands about the same time or a little later. I had a delight in that stupid collection of monkish legends which I cannot account for now, and which persisted in spite of the nightmare confusion it made of my ancient Greeks and Romans. They were not at all the ancient Greeks and Romans of Goldsmith's histories.

I cannot say at what times I read these books, but they must have been odd times, for life was very full of play then, and was already beginning to be troubled

with work.   As I have said, I was to and fro between
the school-house and the printing-office so•much that
when I tired of the one I must have been very
promptly given my choice of the other.   The reading,
however, somehow went on pretty constantly, and no
doubt my love for it won me a chance for it.   There
were some famous cherry-trees in our yard, which, as
I look back at them, seem to have been in flower or
fruit the year round; and in one of them there was a
level branch where a boy could sit with a book till his
dangling legs went to sleep, or till some idler or
busier boy came to the gate and called him down to
play marbles or go swimming.   When this happened
the ancient world was rolled up like a scroll, and put
away until the next day, with all its orators and con-
spirators, its nymphs and satyrs, gods and demigods;
though sometimes they escaped at night and got into
the boy's dreams.

I do not think I cared as much as some of the other
boys for the Arabian Nights or Robinson Crusoe, but
when it came to the Ingenious Gentleman of La
Mancha, I was not only first, I was sole.

Before I speak, however, of the beneficent humorist
who next had my boyish heart after Goldsmith, let
me acquit myself in full of my debt to that not un-

equal or unkindred spirit. I have said it was long
after I had read those histories, full of his inalienable
charm, mere pot-boilers as they were, and far beneath
his more willing efforts, that I came to know his
poetry. My father must have read the Deserted
Village to us, and told us something of the author's
pathetic life, for I cannot remember when I first knew
of "sweet Auburn," or had the light of the poet's own
troubled day upon the "loveliest village of the plain."
The Vicar of Wakefield must have come into my life
after that poem and before The Traveler. It was
when I would have said that I knew all Goldsmith.
We often give ourselves credit for knowledge in this
way without having any tangible assets; and my reading has always been very desultory. I should like to
say here that the reading of any one who reads to
much purpose is always very desultory, but perhaps I
had better not say so, but merely state the fact in my
case, and own that I never read any one author quite
through without wandering from him to others.
When I first read the Vicar of Wakefield, (for I have
since read it several times, and hope yet to read it
many times,) I found its persons and incidents familiar,
and so I suppose I must have heard it read. It is
still for me one of the most modern novels: that is to

say, one of the best. It is unmistakably good up to a certain point, and then unmistakably bad, but with always good enough in it to be forever imperishable. Kindness and gentleness are never out of fashion; it is these in Goldsmith which make him our contemporary, and it is worth the while of any young person presently intending deathless renown to take a little thought of them. They are the source of all refinement, and I do not believe that the best art in any kind exists without them. The style is the man, and he cannot hide himself in any garb of words so that we shall not know somehow what manner of man he is within it; his speech betrayeth him, not only as to his country and his race, but more subtly yet as to his heart, and the loves and hates of his heart. As to Goldsmith, I do not think that a man of harsh and arrogant nature, of worldly and selfish soul, could ever have written his style, and I do think that, in far greater measure than criticism has recognized, his spiritual quality, his essential friendliness, expressed itself in the literary beauty that wins the heart as well as takes the fancy in his work.

I should have my reservations and my animadversions if it came to close criticism of his work, but I am glad that he was the first author I loved, and that

even before I knew I loved him I was his devoted
reader. I was not consciously his admirer till I began
to read, when I was fourteen, a little volume of his
essays, made up, I dare say, from the Citizen of the
World and other unsuccessful ventures of his. It contained the papers on Beau Tibbs, among others, and I
tried to write sketches and studies of life in their
manner. But this attempt at Goldsmith's manner
followed a long time after I tried to write in the style
of Edgar A. Poe, as I knew it from his tales of the
Grotesque and Arabesque. I suppose the very
poorest of these was the Devil in the Belfry, but
such as it was I followed it as closely as I could in
the Devil in the Smoke-Pipes; I meant tobacco-pipes.
The resemblance was noted by those to whom I read
my story; I alone could not see it or would not own
it, and I really felt it a hardship that I should be
found to have produced an imitation.

It was the first time I had imitated a prose writer,
though I had imitated several poets like Moore,
Campbell, and Goldsmith himself. I have never
greatly loved an author without wishing to write like
him. I have now no reluctance to confess that, and I
do not see why I should not say that it was a long
time before I found it best to be as like myself as I

could, even when I did not think so well of myself as
of some others. I hope I shall always be able and
willing to learn something from the masters of literature and still be myself, but for the young writer this
seems impossible. He must form himself from time
to time upon the different authors he is in love with,
but when he has done this he must wish it not to be
known, for that is natural too. The lover always
desires to ignore the object of his passion, and the
adoration which a young writer has for a great one is
truly a passion passing the love of women. I think
it hardly less fortunate that Cervantes was one of my
early passions, though I sat at his feet with no more
sense of his mastery than I had of Goldsmith's.

III

CERVANTES.

I RECALL very fully the moment and the place when I first heard of Don Quixote, while as yet I could not connect it very distinctly with anybody's authorship. I was still too young to conceive of authorship, even in my own case, and wrote my miserable verses without any notion of literature, or of anything but the pleasure of seeing them actually come out rightly rhymed and measured. The moment was at the close of a summer's day just before supper, which, in our house, we had lawlessly late, and the place was the kitchen where my mother was going about her work, and listening as she could to what my father was telling my brother and me and an apprentice of ours, who was like a brother to us both, of a book that he had once read. We boys were all shelling peas, but the story, as it went on, rapt us from the poor employ, and whatever our fingers were doing our spirits

were away in that strange land of adventures and mis-
haps, where the fevered life of the knight truly without fear and without reproach burned itself out.   I
dare say that my father tried to make us understand
the satirical purpose of the book. I vaguely remember
his speaking of the books of chivalry it was meant to
ridicule; but a boy could not care for this, and what
I longed to do at once was to get that book and
plunge into its story.   He told us at random of the
attack on the windmills and the flocks of sheep, of
the night in the valley of the fulling-mills with their
trip-hammers, of the inn and the muleteers, of the
tossing of Sancho in the blanket, of the island that
was given him to govern, and of all the merry pranks
at the duke's and duchess's, of the liberation of the
galley-slaves, of the capture of Mambrino's helmet,
and of Sancho's invention of the enchanted Dulcinea,
and whatever else there was wonderful and delightful in the most wonderful and delightful book in the
world.   I do not know when or where my father got
it for me, and I am aware of an appreciable time
that passed between my hearing of it and my having
it.   The event must have been most important to
me, and it is strange I cannot fix the moment when
the precious story came into my hands; though for

the matter of that there is nothing more capricious than a child's memory, what it will hold and what it will lose.

It is certain my Don Quixote was in two small, stout volumes not much bigger each than my Goldsmith's Greece, bound in a sort of law-calf, well fitted to withstand the wear they were destined to undergo. The translation was, of course, the old-fashioned version of Jervas, which, whether it was a closely faithful version or not, was honest eighteenth-century English, and reported faithfully enough the spirit of the original. If it had any literary influence with me the influence must have been good. But I cannot make out that I was sensible of the literature; it was the forever enchanting story that I enjoyed. I exulted in the boundless freedom of the design; the open air of that immense scene, where adventure followed adventure with the natural sequence of life, and the days and the nights were not long enough for the events that thronged them, amidst the fields and woods, the streams and hills, the highways and byways, hostelries and hovels, prisons and palaces, which were the setting of that matchless history. I took it as simply as I took everything else in the world about me. It was full of meaning that I could not grasp, and there were significances of the kind that literature unhappily abounds in, but they were lost upon my innocence. I did not know whether it was well written or not; I never thought about it; it was simply there in its vast entirety, its inexhaustible opulence, and I was rich in it beyond the dreams of avarice.

My father must have told us that night about Cervantes as well as about his Don Quixote, for I seem to have known from the beginning that he was once a slave in Algiers, and that he had lost a hand in battle, and I loved him with a sort of personal affection, as if he were still living and he could somehow return my love. His name and nature endeared the Spanish name and nature to me, so that they were always my romance, and to this day I cannot meet a Spanish man without clothing him in something of the honor and worship I lavished upon Cervantes when I was a child. While I was in the full flush of this ardor there came to see our school, one day, a Mexican gentleman who was studying the American system of education; a mild, fat, saffron man, whom I could almost have died to please for Cervantes' and Don Quixote's sake, because I knew he spoke their tongue. But he smiled upon us all, and I had no chance to distinguish myself from the rest by any act of devotion before the blessed

vision faded, though for long afterward, in impassioned reveries, I accosted him and claimed him kindred because of my fealty, and because I would have
been Spanish if I could.

I would not have had the boy-world about me know
anything of these fond dreams; and it was my tastes
alone, my passions, which were alien there ; in everything else I was as much a citizen as any boy who had
never heard of Don Quixote.   But I believe that I
carried the book about with me most of the time, so
as not to lose any chance moment of reading it.   Even
in the blank of certain years, when I added little other
reading to my store, I must still have been reading it.
This was after we had removed from the town where
the earlier years of my boyhood were passed, and I
had barely adjusted myself to the strange environment when one of my uncles asked me to come with
him and learn the drug business, in the place, forty
miles away, where he practiced medicine.   We made
the long journey, longer than any I have made since,
in the stage-coach of those days, and we arrived at
his house about twilight, he glad to get home, and I
sick to death with yearning for the home I had left.
I do not know how it was that in this state, when all
the world was one hopeless blackness around me, I

should have got my Don Quixote out of my bag; I
seem to have had it with me as an essential part of
my equipment for my new career. Perhaps I had
been asked to show it, with the notion of beguiling me
from my misery; perhaps I was myself trying to
drown my sorrows in it. But anyhow I have before
me now the vision of my sweet young aunt and her
young sister looking over her shoulder, as they stood
together on the lawn in the summer evening light.
My aunt held my Don Quixote open in one hand,
while she clasped with the other the child she carried
on her arm. She looked at the book, and then from
time to time she looked at me, very kindly but very
curiously, with a faint smile, so that as I stood there,
inwardly writhing in my bashfulness, I had the sense
that in her eyes I was a queer boy. She returned the
book without comment, after some questions, and I
took it off to my room, where the confidential friend
of Cervantes cried himself to sleep.

In the morning I rose up and told them I could not
stand it, and I was going home. Nothing they could
say availed, and my uncle went down to the stage-
office with me and took my passage back.

The horror of cholera was then in the land; and we
heard in the stage-office that a man lay dead of it in

the hotel overhead.   But my uncle led me to his drug-
store, where the stage was to call for me, and made
me taste a little camphor; with this prophylactic, Cervantes and I somehow got home together alive.

The reading of Don Quixote went on throughout
my boyhood, so that I cannot recall any distinctive
period of it when I was not, more or less, reading that
book.   In a boy's way I knew it well when I was ten,
and a few years ago, when I was fifty, I took it up in
the admirable new version of Ormsby, and found it so
full of myself and of my own irrevocable past that I
did not find it very gay.   But I made a great many
discoveries in it; things I had not dreamt of were
there, and must always have been there, and other
things wore a new face, and made a new effect upon
me.   I had my doubts, my reserves, where once I had
given it my whole heart without question, and yet in
what formed the greatness of the book it seemed to
me greater than ever.   I believe that its free and simple design, where event follows event without the
fettering control of intrigue, but where all grows naturally out of character and conditions, is the supreme
form of fiction; and I cannot help thinking that if we
ever have a great American novel it must be built upon some such large and noble lines.   As for the cen-

tral figure, Don Quixote himself, in his dignity and generosity, his unselfish ideals, and his fearless devotion to them, he is always heroic and beautiful; and I was glad to find in my latest look at his history that I had truly conceived of him at first, and had felt the sublimity of his nature. I did not want to laugh at him so much, and I could not laugh at all any more at some of the things done to him. Once they seemed funny, but now only cruel, and even stupid, so that it was strange to realize his qualities and indignities as both flowing from the same mind. But in my mature experience, which threw a broader light on the fable, I was happy to keep my old love of an author who had been almost personally dear to me.

IV.

IRVING.

I HAVE told how Cervantes made his race precious to me, and I am sure that it must have been he who fitted me to understand and enjoy the American author who now stayed me on Spanish ground and kept me happy in Spanish air, though I cannot trace the tie in time and circumstance between Irving and Cervantes. The most I can make sure of is that I read the Conquest of Granada after I read Don Quixote, and that I loved the historian so much because I had loved the novelist much more. Of course I did not perceive then that Irving's charm came largely from Cervantes and the other Spanish humorists yet unknown to me, and that he had formed himself upon them almost as much as upon Goldsmith, but I dare say that this fact had insensibly a great deal to do with my liking. Afterward I came to see it, and at the same time to see what was Irving's own in Irving; to feel his native, if somewhat attenuated humor, and his original, if somewhat too studied grace. But as yet there was no critical question with me. I gave my heart simply and passionately to the author who made the scenes of that most pathetic history live in my sympathy, and companioned me with the stately and gracious actors in them.

I really cannot say now whether I loved the Moors or the Spaniards more. I fought on both sides; I would not have had the Spaniards beaten, and yet when the Moors lost I was vanquished with them; and when the poor young King Boabdil (I was his devoted partisan and at the same time a follower of his fiery old uncle and rival, Hamet el Zegri) heaved the Last Sigh of the Moor, as his eyes left the roofs of Granada forever, it was as much my grief as if it had burst from my own breast. I put both these princes into the first and last historical romance I ever wrote. I have now no idea what they did in it, but as the story never came to a conclusion it does not greatly matter. I had never yet read an historical romance that I can make sure of, and probably my attempt must have been based almost solely upon the facts of Irving's history. I am certain I could not have thought of adding anything to them, or at all varying them.

In reading his Chronicle I suffered for a time from
its attribution to Fray Antonio Agapida, the pious
monk whom he feigns to have written it, just as in
reading Don Quixote I suffered from Cervantes mas-
querading as the Moorish scribe, Cid Hamet Ben En-
geli.   My father explained the literary caprice, but it
remained a confusion and a trouble for me, and I
made a practice of skipping those passages where
either author insisted upon his invention.   I will own
that I am rather glad that sort of thing seems to be
out of fashion now, and I think the directer and frank-
er methods of modern fiction will forbid its revival.
Thackeray was fond of such open disguises, and liked
to greet his reader from the mask of Yellowplush and
Michael Angelo Titmarsh, but it seems to me this was
in his least modern moments.

My Conquest of Granada was in two octavo volumes, bound in drab boards, and printed on paper very
much yellowed with time at its irregular edges.   I do
not know when the books happened in my hands.   I
have no remembrance that they were in anywise offered or commended to me, and in a sort of way they
were as authentically mine as if I had made them.   I
saw them at home, not many months ago, in my father's library (it has long outgrown the old bookcase,

which has gone I know not where), and upon the whole I rather shrank from taking them down, much more from opening them, though I could not say why, unless it was from the fear of perhaps finding the ghost of my boyish self within, pressed flat like a withered leaf, somewhere between the familiar pages.

When I learned Spanish it was with the purpose, never yet fulfilled, of writing the life of Cervantes, although I have since had some forty odd years to do it in. I taught myself the language, or began to do so, when I knew nothing of the English grammar but the prosody at the end of the book. My father had the contempt of familiarity with it, having himself written a very brief sketch of our accidence, and he seems to have let me plunge into the sea of Spanish verbs and adverbs, nouns and pronouns, and all the rest, when as yet I could not confidently call them by name, with the serene belief that if I did not swim I would still somehow get ashore without sinking. The end, perhaps, justified him, and I suppose I did not do all that work without getting some strength from it; but I wish I had back the time that it cost me; I should like to waste it in some other way. However, time seemed interminable then, and I thought there would be enough of it for me in which to read all Spanish literature; or, at least, I did not propose to do anything less.

I followed Irving, too, in my later reading, but at haphazard, and with other authors at the same time. I did my poor best to be amused by his Knickerbocker History of New York, because my father liked it so much, but secretly I found it heavy; and a few years ago when I went carefully through it again I could not laugh. Even as a boy I found some other things of his up-hill work. There was the beautiful manner, but the thought seemed thin; and I do not remember having been much amused by Bracebridge Hall, though I read it devoutly, and with a full sense that it would be very *comme il faut* to like it. But I did like the life of Goldsmith; I liked it a great deal better than the more authoritative life by Forster, and I think there is a deeper and sweeter sense of Goldsmith in it. Better than all, except the Conquest of Granada, I liked the Legend of Sleepy Hollow and the story of Rip Van Winkle, with their humorous and affectionate caricatures of life that was once of our own soil and air; and the Tales of the Alhambra, which transported me again to the scenes of my youth beside the Xenil. It was long after my acquaintance with his work that I came to a due sense of Irving as an artist, and perhaps I have come to feel a full sense of it only now, when I perceive that he worked willingly only when he worked inventively. At last I can do justice to the exquisite conception of his Conquest of Granada, a study of history which, in unique measure, conveys not only the pathos, but the humor of one of the most splendid and impressive situations in the experience of the race. Very possibly something of the severer truth might have been sacrificed to the effect of the pleasing and touching tale, but I do not understand that this was really done. Upon the whole I am very well content with my first three loves in literature, and if I were to choose for any other boy I do not see how I could choose better than Goldsmith and Cervantes and Irving, kindred spirits, and each not a master only, but a sweet and gentle friend, whose kindness could not fail to profit him.

V.

FIRST FICTION AND DRAMA.

In my own case there followed my acquaintance with these authors certain Bœotian years, when if I did not go backward I scarcely went forward in the paths I had set out upon. They were years of the work, of the over-work, indeed, which falls to the lot of so many, that I should be ashamed to speak of it except in accounting for the fact. My father had sold his paper in Hamilton and had bought an interest in another at Dayton, and we were all straining our utmost to help pay for it. My daily tasks began so early and ended so late that I had little time, even if I had the spirit, for reading; and it was not till what we thought ruin, but what was really release, came to us that I got back again to my books. Then we went to live in the country for a year, and that stress of toil, with the shadow of failure darkening all, fell from me like the horror of an evil dream. The only new book which I remember to have read in those two or three

years at Dayton, when I hardly remember to have
read any old ones, was the novel of Jane Eyre, which
I took in very imperfectly, and which I associate with
the first rumor of the Rochester Knockings, then just
beginning to reverberate through a world that they
have not since left wholly at peace. It was a gloomy
Sunday afternoon when the book came under my
hand; and mixed with my interest in the story was
an anxiety lest the pictures on the walls should
leave their nails and come and lay themselves at my
feet; that was what the pictures had been doing in
Rochester and other places where the disembodied spirits were beginning to make themselves felt. The thing
did not really happen in my case, but I was alone in
the house, and it might very easily have happened.

If very little came to me in those days from books,
on the other hand, my acquaintance with the drama
vastly enlarged itself. There was a hapless company
of players in the town from time to time, and they
came to us for their printing. I believe they never
paid for it, or at least never wholly, but they lavished
free passes upon us, and as nearly as I can make out,
at this distance of time, I profited by their generosity every night. They gave two or three plays
at every performance to houses ungratefully small,

but of a lively spirit and impatient temper that would not brook delay in the representation; and they changed the bill each day. In this way I became familiar with Shakespeare before I read him, or at least such plays of his as were most given in those days, and I saw Macbeth and Hamlet, and above all Richard III., again and again. I do not know why my delight in those tragedies did not send me to the volume of his plays, which was all the time in the bookcase at home, but I seem not to have thought of it, and rapt as I was in them I am not sure that they gave me greater pleasure, or seemed at all finer, than Rollo, The Wife, The Stranger, Barbarossa, The Miser of Marseilles, and the rest of the melo-dramas, comedies and farces that I saw at that time. I have a notion that there were some clever people in one of these companies, and that the lighter pieces at least were well played, but I may be altogether wrong. The gentleman who took the part of villain, with an unfailing love of evil, in the different dramas, used to come about the printing-office a good deal, and I was puzzled to find him a very mild and gentle person. To be sure he had a mustache, which in those days devoted a man to wickedness, but by day it was a blond mustache, quite flaxen, in fact, and not at all

the dark and deadly thing it was behind the foot-
lights at night. I could scarcely gasp in his presence,
my heart bounded so in awe and honor of him when
he paid a visit to us; perhaps he used to bring the
copy of the showbills. The company he belonged to
left town in the adversity habitual with them.

Our own adversity had been growing, and now it
became overwhelming. We had to give up the paper
we had struggled so hard to keep, but when the worst
came it was not half so bad as what had gone
before. There was no more waiting till midnight for
the telegraphic news, no more waking at dawn to
deliver the papers, no more weary days at the case,
heavier for the doom hanging over us. My father
and his brothers had long dreamed of a sort of family
colony somewhere in the country, and now the uncle
who was most prosperous bought a milling property
on a river not far from Dayton, and my father went
out to take charge of it until the others could shape
their business to follow him. The scheme came to
nothing finally, but in the meantime we escaped from
the little city and its sorrowful associations of fruitless
labor, and had a year in the country, which was
blest, at least to us children, by sojourn in a log-
cabin, while a house was building for us.

VI.

LONGFELLOW'S SPANISH STUDENT.

This log-cabin had a loft, where we boys slept, and in the loft were stored in barrels the books that had now begun to overflow the bookcase. I do not know why I chose the loft to renew my long-neglected friendship with them. The light could not have been good, though if I brought my books to the little gable window that overlooked the groaning and whistling gristmill I could see well enough. But perhaps I liked the loft best because the books were handiest there, and because I could be alone. At any rate, it was there that I read Longfellow's Spanish Student, which I found in an old paper copy of his poems in one of the barrels, and I instantly conceived for it the passion which all things Spanish inspired in me. As I read I not only renewed my acquaintance with literature, but renewed my delight in people and places where I had been happy before those heavy years in Dayton. At the same time I felt a little jealousy, a little grudge, that any one else should love them as well as I, and if the poem had not been so beautiful I should have hated the poet for trespassing on my ground. But I could not hold out long against the witchery of his verse. The Spanish Student became one of my passions ; a minor passion, not a grand one, like Don Quixote and the Conquest of Granada, but still a passion, and I should dread a little to read the piece now, lest I should disturb my old ideal of its beauty. The hero's rogue servant, Chispa, seemed to me, then and long afterward, so fine a bit of Spanish character that I chose his name for my first pseudonym when I began to write for the newspapers, and signed my legislative correspondence for a Cincinnati paper with it. I was in love with the heroine, the lovely dancer whose *cachucha* turned my head, along with that of the cardinal, but whose name even I have forgotten, and I went about with the thought of her burning in my heart, as if she had been a real person.

VII.

SCOTT.

ALL the while I was bringing up the long arrears of play which I had not enjoyed in the toil-years at Dayton, and was trying to make my Spanish reading serve in the sports that we had in the woods and by the river. We were Moors and Spaniards almost as often as we were British and Americans, or settlers and Indians. I suspect that the large, mild boy, the son of a neighboring farmer, who mainly shared our games, had but a dim notion of what I meant by my strange people, but I did my best to enlighten him, and he helped me make a dream out of my life, and did his best to dwell in the region of unrealities where I preferably had my being; he was from time to time a Moor when I think he would rather have been a Mingo.

I got hold of Scott's poems, too, in that cabin loft, and read most of the tales which were yet unknown to me after those earlier readings of my father's. I could not say why Harold the Dauntless most took my fancy; the fine, strongly-flowing rhythm of the verse had a good deal to do with it, I believe. I liked these things, all of them, and in after years I liked the Lady of the Lake more and more, and from mere love of it got great lengths of it by heart; but I cannot say that Scott was then or ever a great passion with me. It was a sobered affection at best, which came from my sympathy with his love of nature, and the whole kindly and humane keeping of his genius. Many years later, during the month when I was waiting for my passport as Consul for Venice, and had the time on my hands, I passed it chiefly in reading all his novels, one after another, without the interruption of other reading. Ivanhoe I had known before, and the Bride of Lammermoor and Woodstock, but the rest had remained in that sort of abeyance which is often the fate of books people expect to read as a matter of course, and come very near not reading at all, or read only very late. Taking them in this swift sequence, little or nothing of them remained with me, and my experience with them is against that sort of ordered and regular reading, which I have so often heard advised for young people by their elders. I always suspect their elders of not having done that kind of reading themselves.

For my own part I believe I have never got any good from a book that I did not read lawlessly and willfully, out of all leading and following, and merely because I wanted to read it; and I here make bold to praise that way of doing. The book which you read from a sense of duty, or because for any reason you must, does not commonly make friends with you. It may happen that it will yield you an unexpected delight, but this will be in its own unentreated way and in spite of your good intentions. Little of the book read for a purpose stays with the reader, and this is one reason why reading for review is so vain and unprofitable. I have done a vast deal of this, but I have usually been aware that the book was subtly withholding from me the best a book can give, since I was not reading it for its own sake and because I loved it, but for selfish ends of my own, and because I wished to possess myself of it for business purposes, as it were. The reading that does one good, and lasting good, is the reading that one does for pleasure, and simply and unselfishly, as children do. Art will still withhold herself from thrift, and she does well, for nothing but love has any right to her.

Little remains of the events of any period, however vivid they were in passing. The memory may hold record of everything, as it is believed, but it will not be easily entreated to give up its facts, and I find myself striving in vain to recall the things that I must have read that year in the country. Probably I read the old things over; certainly I kept on with Cervantes, and very likely with Goldsmith. There was a delightful history of Ohio, stuffed with tales of the pioneer times, which was a good deal in the hands of us boys; and there was a book of Western Adventure, full of Indian fights and captivities, which we wore to pieces. Still, I think that it was now that I began to have a literary sense of what I was reading. I wrote a diary, and I tried to give its record form and style, but mostly failed. The versifying which I was always at was easier, and yielded itself more to my hand. I should be very glad to know at present what it dealt with.

VIII.

When my uncles changed their minds in regard to colonizing their families at the mills, as they did in about a year, it became necessary for my father to look about for some new employment, and he naturally looked in the old direction. There were several schemes for getting hold of this paper and that, and there were offers that came to nothing. In that day there were few salaried editors in the country outside of New York, and the only hope we could have was of some place as printers in an office which we might finally buy. The affair ended in our going to the State capital, where my father found work as a reporter of legislative proceedings for one of the daily journals, and I was taken into the office as a compositor. In this way I came into living contact with literature again, and the day-dreams began once more over the familiar cases of type. A definite literary ambition grew up in me, and in the long reveries of the afternoon, when I was distributing my case, I fashioned a future of overpowering magnificence and undying celebrity. I should be ashamed to say what literary triumphs I achieved in those preposterous deliriums. What I actually did was to write a good many copies of verse, in imitation, never owned, of Moore and Goldsmith, and some minor poets, whose work caught my fancy, as I read it in the newspapers or put it into type.

One of my pieces, which fell so far short of my visionary performances as to treat of the lowly and familiar theme of Spring, was the first thing I ever had in print. My father offered it to the editor of the paper I worked on, and I first knew, with mingled shame and pride, of what he had done when I saw it in the journal. In the tumult of my emotions I promised myself that if I got through this experience safely I would never suffer anything else of mine to be published ; but it was not long before I offered the editor a poem myself. I am now glad to think it dealt with so humble a fact as a farmer's family leaving their old home for the West. The only fame of my poem which reached me was when another boy in the office quoted some lines of it in derision. This covered me with such confusion that I wonder that I did not vanish from the earth. At the same time I had my secret joy in it, and even yet I think it was attempted in a way which was not false or wrong. I had tried to sketch an aspect of life that I had seen and known, and that was very well indeed, and I had wrought patiently and carefully in the art of the poor little affair.

My elder brother, for whom there was no place in the office where I worked, had found one in a store, and he beguiled the leisure that a light trade left on his hands by reading the novels of Captain Marryat. I read them after him with a great deal of amusement, but without the passion that I bestowed upon my favorite authors. I believe I had no critical reserves in regard to them, but simply they did not take my fancy. Still, we had great fun with Japhet in Search of a Father, and with Midshipman Easy, and we felt a fine psychical shiver in the darkling moods of Snarleyow the Dog-Fiend. I do not remember even the names of the other novels, except Jacob Faithful, which I chanced upon a few years ago and found very hard reading.

We children who were used to the free range of woods and fields were homesick for the country in our narrow city yard, and I associate with this longing the

Farmer Boy of Bloomfield, which my father got for me. It was a little book in blue cloth, and there were some mild woodcuts in it. I read it with a tempered pleasure, and with a vague resentment of its trespass upon Thomson's ground in the division of its parts under the names of the seasons. I do not know why I need have felt this. I was not yet very fond of Thomson. I really liked Bloomfield better; for one thing, his poem was written in the heroic decasyllabics which I preferred to any other verse.

IX.

POPE.

I INFER from the fact of this preference that I had already begun to read Pope, and that I must have read the Deserted Village of Goldsmith. I fancy, also, that I must by this time have read the Odyssey, for the Battle of the Frogs and Mice was in the second volume, and it took me so much that I paid it the tribute of a bald imitation in a mock-heroic epic of a cat fight, studied from the cat fights in our back yard, with the wonted invocation to the Muse, and the machinery of partisan gods and goddesses. It was in some hundreds of verses, which I did my best to balance as Pope did, with a cæsura falling in the middle of the line, and a neat antithesis at either end.

The story of the Odyssey charmed me, of course, and I had moments of being intimate friends with Ulysses, but I was passing out of that phase, and was coming to read more with a sense of the author, and

less with a sense of his characters as real persons;
that is, I was growing more literary, and less human.
I fell in love with Pope, whose life I read with an ardor of sympathy which I am afraid he hardly merited.
I was of his side in all his quarrels, as far as I understood them, and if I did not understand them I was
of his side anyway. When I found that he was a
Catholic I was almost ready to abjure the Protestant
religion for his sake; but I perceived that this was
not necessary when I came to know that most of his
friends were Protestants. If the truth must be told,
I did not like his best things at first, but long remained chiefly attached to his rubbishing pastorals,
which I was perpetually imitating, with a whole ap-
paratus of swains and shepherdesses, purling brooks,
enameled meads, rolling years, and the like.

After my day's work at the case I toiled the evening away at my boyish literary attempts, forcing my
poor invention in that unnatural kind, and rubbing
and polishing at my wretched verses till they did
sometimes take on an effect, which, if it was not like
Pope's, was like none of mine. With all my pains I
do not think I ever managed to bring any of my pastorals to a satisfactory close. They all stopped somewhere about half way. My swains could not think of

anything more to say, and the merits of my shepherd-esses remained undecided. To this day I do not know whether in any given instance it was the champion of Chloe or of Sylvia that carried off the prize for his fair, but I dare say it does not much matter. I am sure that I produced a rhetoric as artificial and treated of things as unreal as my master in the art, and I am rather glad that I acquainted myself so thoroughly with a mood of literature, which, whatever we may say against it, seems to have expressed very perfectly a mood of civilization.

The severe schooling I gave myself was not without its immediate use. I learned how to choose between words after a study of their fitness, and though I often employed them decoratively and with no vital sense of their qualities, still in mere decoration they had to be chosen intelligently, and after some thought about their structure and meaning. I could not imi-tate Pope without imitating his methods, and his method was to the last degree intelligent. He cer-tainly knew what he was doing, and although I did not always know what I was doing, he made me wish to know, and ashamed of not knowing. There are several truer poets who might not have done this; and after all the modern contempt of Pope, he seems to me to have been at least one of the great masters, if not one of the great poets. The poor man's life was as weak and crooked as his frail, tormented body, but he had a dauntless spirit, and he fought his way against odds that might well have appalled a stronger nature. I suppose I must own that he was from time to time a snob, and from time to time a liar, but I believe that he loved the truth, and would have liked always to respect himself if he could. He violently revolted, now and again, from the abasement to which he forced himself, and he always bit the heel that trod on him, especially if it was a very high, narrow heel, with a clocked stocking and a hooped skirt above it. I loved him fondly at one time, and afterwards despised him, but now I am not sorry for the love, and I am very sorry for the despite. I humbly own a vast debt to him, not the least part of which is the perception that he is a model of ever so much more to be shunned than to be followed in literature.

He was the first of the writers of great Anna's time whom I knew, and he made me ready to understand, if he did not make me understand at once, the order of mind and life which he belonged to. Thanks to his pastorals, I could long afterwards enjoy with the double sense requisite for full pleasure in them, such

divinely excellent artificialties as Tasso's Aminta and
Guarini's Pastor Fido; things which you will thoroughly like only after you are in the joke of thinking
how people once seriously liked them as high exam-
ples of poetry.

Of course I read other things of Pope's besides his
pastorals, even at the time I read these so much. I
read, or not very easily or willingly read at, his Essay
on Man, which my father admired, and which he
probably put Pope's works into my hands to have me
read; and I read the Dunciad, with quite a furious ardor in the tiresome quarrels it celebrates, and an interest in its machinery, which it fatigues me to think of.
But it was only a few years ago that I read the Rape
of the Lock, a thing perfect of its kind, whatever we
may choose to think of the kind. Upon the whole I
think much better of the kind than I once did, though
still not so much as I should have thought if I had
read the poem when the fever of my love for Pope
was at the highest.

It is a nice question how far one is helped or hurt
by one's idealizations of historical or imaginary characters, and I shall not try to answer it fully. I suppose that if I once cherished such a passion for Pope
personally that I would willingly have done the things

that he did, and told the lies, and vented the malice, and inflicted the cruelties that the poor soul was full of, it was for the reason, partly, that I did not see these things as they were, and that in the glamour of his talent I was blind to all but the virtues of his defects, which he certainly had, and partly that in my love of him I could not take sides against him, even when I knew him to be wrong. After all, I fancy not much harm comes to the devoted boy from his enthusiasms for this imperfect hero or that. In my own case I am sure that I distinguished as to certain sins in my idols. I could not cast them down or cease to worship them, but some of their frailties grieved me and put me to secret shame for them. I did not excuse these things in them, or try to believe that they were less evil for them than they would have been for less people. This was after I came more or less to the knowledge of good and evil. While I remained in the innocence of childhood I did not even understand the wrong. When I realized what lives some of my poets had led, how they were drunkards, and swindlers, and unchaste, and untrue, I lamented over them with a sense of personal disgrace in them, and to this day I have no patience with that code of the world which relaxes itself in behalf of the brilliant and gifted offender; rather he should suffer more blame. The worst of the literature of past times, before an ethical conscience began to inform it, or the advance of the race compelled it to decency, is that it leaves the mind foul with filthy images and base thoughts; but what I have been trying to say is that the boy, unless he is exceptionally depraved beforehand, is saved from these through his ignorance. Still I wish they were not there, and I hope the time will come when the beast-man will be so far subdued and tamed in us that the memory of him in literature shall be left to perish; that what is lewd and ribald in the great poets shall be kept out of such editions as are meant for general reading, and that the pedant-pride which now perpetuates it as an essential part of those poets shall no longer have its way. At the end of the ends such things do defile, they do corrupt. We may palliate them or excuse them for this reason or that, but that is the truth, and I do not see why they should not be dropped from literature, as they were long ago dropped from the talk of decent people. The literary histories might keep record of them, but it is loathsome to think of those heaps of ordure, accumulated from generation to generation, and carefully passed down from age to age as something precious and vital,

and not justly regarded as the moral offal which they
are.

During the winter we passed at Columbus I suppose
that my father read things aloud to us after his old
habit, and that I listened with the rest. I have a dim
notion of first knowing Thomson's Castle of Indolence
in this way, but I was getting more and more impatient of having things read to me. The trouble was
that I caught some thought or image from the text,
and that my fancy remained playing with that while
the reading went on, and I lost the rest. But I think
the reading was less in every way than it had been,
because his work was exhausting and his leisure less.
My own hours in the printing-office began at seven
and ended at six, with an hour at noon for dinner,
which I often used for putting down such verses as
had come to me during the morning. As soon as
supper was over at night I got out my manuscripts,
which I kept in great disorder, and written in several
different hands on several different kinds of paper, and
sawed, and filed, and hammered away at my blessed
Popean heroics till nine, when I went regularly to bed,
to rise again at five. Sometimes the foreman gave
me an afternoon off on Saturdays, and though the
days were long the work was not always constant, and

was never very severe. I suspect now the office was
not so prosperous as might have been wished. I was
shifted from place to place in it, and there was plenty
of time for my day-dreams over the distribution of my
case. I was very fond of my work, though, and proud
of my swiftness and skill in it. Once when the perplexed foreman could not think of any task to set me
he offered me a holiday, but I would not take it, so I
fancy that at this time I was not more interested in
my art of poetry than in my trade of printing. What
went on in the office interested me as much as the
quarrels of the Augustan age of English letters, and I
made much more record of it in the crude and shape-
less diary which I kept, partly in verse and partly in
prose, but always of a distinctly lower literary kind
than that I was trying otherwise to write.

There must have been some mention in it of the
tremendous combat with wet sponges I saw there one
day between two of the boys who hurled them back
and forth at each other. This amiable fray, carried
on during the foreman's absence, forced upon my notice for the first time the boy who has come to be a
name well-known in literature. I admired his vigor
as a combatant, but I never spoke to him at that time,
and I never dreamed that he, too, was effervescing

with verse, probably as fiercely as myself. Six or seven years later we met again, when we had both become journalists, and had both had poems accepted by Mr. Lowell for the Atlantic Monthly, and then we formed a literary friendship which eventuated in the joint publication of a volume of verse. The Poems of Two Friends became instantly and lastingly unknown to fame; the West waited, as it always does, to hear what the East should say; the East said nothing, and two-thirds of the small edition of five hundred came back upon the publisher's hands. I imagine these copies were " ground up " in the manner of worthless stock, for I saw a single example of the book quoted the other day in a book-seller's catalogue at ten dollars, and I infer that it is so rare as to be prized at least for its rarity. It was a very pretty little book, printed on tinted paper then called " blush," in the trade, and it was manufactured in the same office where we had once been boys together, unknown to each other. Another boy of that time had by this time become foreman in the office, and he was very severe with us about the proofs, and sent us hurting messages on the margin. Perhaps he thought we might be going to take on airs, and perhaps we might have taken on airs if the fate of our book had been different. As it was

I really think we behaved with sufficient meekness, and after thirty four or five years for reflection I am still of a very modest mind about my share of the book, in spite of the price it bears in the book-seller's catalogue. But I have steadily grown in liking for my friend's share in it, and I think that there is at present no American of twenty-three writing verse of so good a quality, with an ideal so pure and high, and from an impulse so authentic as John J. Piatt's were then. He already knew how to breathe into his glowing rhyme the very spirit of the region where we were both native, and in him the Middle West has its true poet, who was much more than its poet, who had a rich and tender imagination, a lovely sense of color, and a touch even then securely and fully his own. I was reading over his poems in that poor little book a few days ago, and wondering with shame and contrition that I had not at once known their incomparable superiority to mine. But I used then and for long afterward to tax him with obscurity, not knowing that my own want of simplicity and directness was to blame for that effect.

My reading from the first was such as to enamour me of clearness, of definiteness; anything left in the vague was intolerable to me; but my long subjection to Pope, while it was useful in other ways, made me

so strictly literary in my point of view that sometimes
I could not see what was, if more naturally approached
and without any technical preoccupation, perfectly
transparent. It remained for another great passion,
perhaps the greatest of my life, to fuse these gyves in
which I was trying so hard to dance, and free me forever from the bonds which I had spent so much time
and trouble to involve myself in. But I was not to
know that passion for five or six years yet, and in the
meantime I kept on as I had been going, and worked
out my deliverance in the predestined way. What I
liked then was regularity, uniformity, exactness. I
did not conceive of literature as the expression of
life, and I could not imagine that it ought to be desultory, mutable and unfixed, even if at the risk of some
vagueness.

X.

VARIOUS PREFERENCES.

My father was very fond of Byron, and I must before this have known that his poems were in our bookcase. While we were still in Columbus I began to read them, but I did not read so much of them as could have helped me to a truer and freer ideal. I read English Bards and Scotch Reviewers, and I liked its vulgar music and its heavy-handed sarcasm. These would, perhaps, have fascinated any boy, but I had such a fanaticism for methodical verse that any variation from the octosyllabic and decasyllabic couplets was painful to me. The Spencerian stanza, with its rich variety of movement and its harmonious closes, long shut Childe Harold from me, and whenever I found a poem in any book which did not rhyme its second line with its first I read it unwillingly or not at all.

This craze could not last, of course, but it lasted beyond our stay in Columbus, which ended with the winter, when the Legislature adjourned, and my father's employment ceased. He tried to find some editorial work on the paper which had printed his reports, but every place was full, and it was hopeless to dream of getting a proprietary interest in it. We had nothing, and we must seek a chance where something besides money would avail us. This offered itself in the village of Ashtabula, in the northeastern part of the State, and there we all found ourselves one moonlight night of early summer. The Lake Shore Railroad then ended at Ashtabula, in a bank of sand, and my elder brother and I walked up from the station, while the rest of the family, which pretty well filled the omnibus, rode. We had been very happy at Columbus, as we were apt to be anywhere, but none of us liked the narrowness of city streets, even so near to the woods as those were, and we were eager for the country again. We had always lived hitherto in large towns, except for that year at the Mills, and we were eager to see what a village was like, especially a village peopled wholly by Yankees, as our father had reported it. I must own that we found it far prettier than anything we had known in Southern Ohio, which we were so fond of and so loath to leave, and as I look back it still seems to me one of the prettiest little places I have ever known, with its white wooden houses, glimmering in the dark of its elms and maples, and their silent gardens beside each, and the silent, grass-bordered, sandy streets between them. The hotel, where we rejoined our family, lurked behind a group of lofty elms, and we drank at the town pump before it just for the pleasure of pumping it.

The village was all that we could have imagined of simply and sweetly romantic in the moonlight, and when the day came it did not rob it of its charm. It was as lovely in my eyes as the loveliest village of the plain, and it had the advantage of realizing the Deserted Village without being deserted.

XI.

UNCLE TOM'S CABIN.

THE book that moved me most, in our stay of six months at Ashtabula, was then beginning to move the whole world more than any other book has moved it. I read it as it came out week after week in the old National Era, and I broke my heart over Uncle Tom's Cabin, as every one else did. Yet I cannot say that it was a passion of mine like Don Quixote, or the other books that I have loved intensely. I felt its greatness when I read it first, and as often as I have read it since, I have seen more and more clearly that it is a very great novel. With certain obvious lapses in its art, and with an art that is at its best very simple, and perhaps primitive, the book is still a work of art. I knew this, in a measure then, as I know it now, and yet neither the literary pride I was beginning to have in the perception of such things, nor the powerful appeal it made to my sympathies, sufficed to impassion me of it. I could not say why this was so. Why does the young man's fancy, when it lightly turns to thoughts of love, turn this way and not that? There seems no more reason for one than for the other.

Instead of remaining steeped to the lips in the strong interest of what is still perhaps our chief fiction, I shed my tribute of tears, and went on my way. I did not try to write a story of slavery, as I might very well have done; I did not imitate either the make or the manner of Mrs. Stowe's romance; I kept on at my imitation of Pope's pastorals, which I dare say I thought much finer, and worthier the powers of such a poet as I meant to be. I did this, as I must have felt then, at some personal risk of a supernatural kind, for my studies were apt to be prolonged into the night after the rest of the family had gone to bed, and a certain ghost, which I had every reason to fear, might very well have visited the small room given me to write in. There was a story, which I shrank from verifying, that a former inmate of our house had hung himself in it, but I do not know to this day whether it was true or not. The doubt did not prevent him from dangling at the door-post, in my consciousness, and many a time I shunned the sight of this problematical suicide by keeping my eyes fastened on the book before me. It was a very simple device, but perfectly effective, as I think any one will find who employs it in like circumstances; and I would really like to commend it to growing boys troubled as I was then.

I never heard who the poor soul was, or why he took himself out of the world, if he really did so, or if he ever was in it; but I am sure that my passion for Pope, and my purpose of writing pastorals must have been powerful indeed to carry me through dangers of that kind. I suspect that the strongest proof of their existence was the gloomy and ruinous look of the house, which was one of the oldest in the village, and the only one that was for rent, there. We went into it because we must, and we were to leave it as soon as we could find a better. But before this happened we left Ashtabula, and I parted with one of the few possibilities I have enjoyed of seeing a ghost on his own ground, as it were.

I was not sorry, for I believe I never went in or came out of the place, by day or by night, without a shudder, more or less secret; and at least, now, we should be able to get another house.

XII.

VERY likely the reading of Ossian had something to do with my morbid anxieties. I had read Byron's imitation of him before that, and admired it prodigiously, and when my father got me the book—as usual I did not know where or how he got it—not all the tall forms that moved before the eyes of haunted bards in the dusky vale of autumn could have kept me from it. There were certain outline illustrations in it, which were very good in the cold Flaxman manner, and helped largely to heighten the fascination of the poems for me. They did not supplant the pastorals of Pope in my affections, and they were never the grand passion with me that Pope's poems had been.

I began at once to make my imitations of Ossian, and I dare say they were not windier and mistier than the original. At the same time I read the literature of the subject, and gave the pretensions of Macpherson an unquestioning faith. I should have made very short work of any one who had impugned the authenticity of the poems, but happily there was no one who held the contrary opinion in that village, so far as I knew, or who cared for Ossian, or had even heard of him. This saved me a great deal of heated controversy with my contemporaries, but I had it out in many angry reveries with Dr. Johnson and others, who had dared to say in their time that the poems of Ossian were not genuine lays of the Gaelic bard, handed down from father to son, and taken from the lips of old women in Highland huts, as Macpherson claimed.

In fact I lived over in my small way the epoch of the eighteenth century in which these curious frauds found polite acceptance all over Europe, and I think yet that they were really worthier of acceptance than most of the artificialities that then passed for poetry. There was a light of nature in them, and this must have been what pleased me, so long shut up to the studio-work of Pope. But strangely enough I did not falter in my allegiance to him, or realize that here in this free form was a deliverance, if I liked, from the fetters and manacles which I had been at so much

pains to fit myself with. Probably nothing would then
have persuaded me to put them off, permanently, or to
do more than lay them aside for the moment while I
tried that new stop and that new step.

I think that even then I had an instinctive doubt
whether formlessness was really better than formality.
Something, it seems to me, may be contained and
kept alive in formality, but in formlessness everything
spills and wastes away. This is what I find the fatal
defect of our American Ossian, Walt Whitman, whose
way is where artistic madness lies. He had great
moments, beautiful and noble thoughts, generous as-
pirations, and a heart wide and warm enough for the
whole race, but he had no bounds, no shape; he was
as liberal as the casing air, but he was often as vague
and intangible. I cannot say how long my passion
for Ossian lasted, but not long, I fancy, for I cannot
find any trace of it in the time following our removal
from Ashtabula to the county seat at Jefferson. I
kept on with Pope, I kept on with Cervantes, I kept
on with Irving, but I suppose there was really not
substance enough in Ossian to feed my passion, and
it died of inanition.

XIII.

SHAKESPEARE.

THE establishment of our paper in the village where there had been none before, and its enlargement from four to eight pages, were events so filling that they left little room for any other excitement but that of getting acquainted with the young people of the village, and going to parties, and sleigh rides, and walks, and drives, and picnics, and dances, and all the other pleasures which that community seemed to indulge beyond any other we had known. The village was smaller than the one we had just left, but it was by no means less lively, and I think that for its size and time and place it had an uncommon share of what has since been called culture. The intellectual experience of the people was mainly theological and political, as it was everywhere in that day, but there were several among them who had a real love for books, and when they met at the druggist's, as they did every night, to dispute of the inspiration of the scriptures and the principles of the Free Soil party, the talk sometimes turned upon the respective merits of Dickens and Thackeray, Gibbon and Macaulay, Wordsworth and Byron. There were law students who read Noctes Ambrosianæ, the Age of Reason, and Bailey's Festus, as well as Blackstone's Commentaries; and there was a public library in that village of six hundred people, small but very well selected, which was kept in one of the lawyers' offices, and was free to all. It seems to me now that the people met there oftener than they do in most country places, and rubbed their wits together more, but this may be one of those pleasing illusions of memory which men in later life are subject to.

I insist upon nothing, but certainly the air was friendlier to the tastes I had formed than any I had yet known, and I found a wider if not deeper sympathy with them. There was one of our printers who liked books, and we went through Don Quixote together again, and through the Conquest of Granada, and we began to read other things of Irving's. There was a very good little stock of books at the village drugstore, and among those that began to come into my hands were the poems of Dr. Holmes, stray volumes of De Quincey, and here and there minor works of Thackeray's. I believe I had no money to buy them, but there was an open account, or a comity, between the printer and the bookseller, and I must have been allowed a certain discretion in regard to getting books.

Still, I do not think I went far in the more modern authors, or gave my heart to any of them. Suddenly, it was now given to Shakespeare, without notice or reason, that I can recall, except that my friend liked him too, and that we found it a double pleasure to read him together. Printers in the old-time offices were always spouting Shakespeare more or less, and I suppose I could not have kept away from him much longer in the nature of things. I cannot fix the time or place when my friend and I began to read him, but it was in the fine print of that unhallowed edition of ours, and presently we had great lengths of him by heart, out of Hamlet, out of the Tempest, out of Macbeth, out of Richard III., out of Midsummer-Night's Dream, out of the Comedy of Errors, out of Julius Cæsar, out of Measure for Measure, out of Romeo and Juliet, out of Two Gentlemen of Verona.

These were the plays that we loved, and must have read in common, or at least at the same time: but others that I more especially liked were the Histories, and among them particularly the Henrys, where Falstaff appeared. This gross and palpable reprobate greatly took my fancy. I delighted in him immensely, and in his comrades, Pistol, and Bardolph, and Nym. I could not read of his death without emotion, and it was a personal pang to me when the prince, crowned king, denied him: blackguard for blackguard, I still think the prince the worse blackguard. Perhaps I flatter myself, but I believe that even then, as a boy of sixteen, I fully conceived of Falstaff's character, and entered into the author's wonderfully humorous conception of him. There is no such perfect conception of the selfish sensualist in literature, and the conception is all the more perfect because of the wit that lights up the vice of Falstaff, a cold light without tenderness, for he was not a good fellow, though a merry companion. I am not sure but I should put him beside Hamlet, and on the same level, for the merit of his artistic completeness, and at one time I much preferred him, or at least his humor.

As to Falstaff personally, or his like, I was rather fastidious, and would not have made friends with him in the flesh, much or little. I reveled in all his appearances in the Histories, and I tried to be as happy where a factitious and perfunctory Falstaff comes to life again in the Merry Wives of Windsor, though at the bottom of my heart I felt the difference. I began to make my imitations of Shakespeare, and I wrote out passages where Falstaff and Pistol and Bardolph talked together, in that Ercles vein which is so easily caught. This was after a year or two of the irregular and interrupted acquaintance with the author which has been my mode of friendship with all the authors I have loved. My worship of Shakespeare went to heights and lengths that it had reached with no earlier idol, and there was a supreme moment, once, when I found myself saying that the creation of Shakespeare was as great as the creation of a planet.

There ought certainly to be some bound beyond which the cult of favorite authors should not be suffered to go. I should keep well within the limit of that early excess now, and should not liken the creation of Shakespeare to the creation of any heavenly body bigger, say, than one of the nameless asteroids that revolve between Mars and Jupiter. Even this I do not feel to be a true means of comparison, and I think that in the case of all great men we like to let our wonder mount and mount, till it leaves the truth behind, and honesty is pretty much cast out for ballast. A wise criticism will no more magnify Shakespeare because he is already great than it will magnify any less man. But we are loaded down with the responsibility of finding him all we have been told he is, and we must do this or suspect ourselves of a want of taste, a want of sensibility. At the same time, we may really be honester than those who have led us to expect this or that of him, and more truly his friends. I wish the time might come when we could read Shakespeare, and Dante, and Homer, as sincerely and as fairly as we read any new book by the least known of our contemporaries. The course of criticism is toward this, but when I began to read Shakespeare I should not have ventured to think that he was not at every moment great. I should no more have thought of questioning the poetry of any passage in him than of questioning the proofs of holy writ. All the same, I knew very well that much which I read was really poor stuff, and the persons and positions were often preposterous. It is a great pity that the ardent youth should not be permitted and even encouraged to say this to himself, instead of falling slavishly before a great author and accepting him at all points as infallible. Shakespeare is fine enough and great enough when all the possible detractions are made, and I have no fear of saying now that he would be finer and greater for the loss of half his work, though if I had heard any one say such a thing then I should have held him as little better than one of the wicked.

Upon the whole it was well that I had not found my way to Shakespeare earlier, though it is rather strange that I had not. I knew him on the stage in most of the plays that used to be given. I had shared the conscience of Macbeth, the passion of Othello, the doubt of Hamlet; many times, in my natural affinity for villains, I had mocked and suffered with Richard III.

Probably no dramatist ever needed the stage less, and none ever brought more to it. There have been few joys for me in life comparable to that of seeing the curtain rise on Hamlet, and hearing the guards begin to talk about the ghost; and yet how fully this joy imparts itself without any material embodiment! It is the same in the whole range of his plays: they fill the scene, but if there is no scene they fill the soul. They are neither worse nor better because of the theatre. They are so great that it cannot hamper them; they are so vital that they enlarge it to their own proportions and endue it with something of their own

living force. They make it the size of life, and yet
they retire it so wholly that you think no more of it
than you think of the physiognomy of one who talks
importantly to you. I have heard people say that they
would rather not see Shakespeare played than to see
him played ill, but I cannot agree with them. He can
better afford to be played ill than any other man that
ever wrote. Whoever is on the stage it is always
Shakespeare who is speaking to me, and perhaps this
is the reason why in the past I can trace no discrep-
ancy between reading his plays and seeing them.

The effect is so equal from either experience that I
am not sure as to some plays whether I read them or
saw them first, though as to most of them I am aware
that I never saw them at all; and if the whole truth
must be told there is still one of his plays that I have
not read, and I believe it is esteemed one of his greatest. There are several, with all my reading of others,
that I had not read till within a few years; and I do
not think I should have lost much if I had never read
Pericles and Winter's Tale.

In those early days I had no philosophized preference for reality in literature, and I dare say if I had
been asked, I should have said that the plays of
Shakespeare where reality is least felt were the most

'imaginative; that is the belief of the puerile critics still; but I suppose it was my instinctive liking for reality that made the great Histories so delightful to me, and that rendered Macbeth and Hamlet vital in their very ghosts and witches. There I found a world appreciable to experience, a world inexpressibly vaster and grander than the poor little affair that I had only known a small obscure corner of, and yet of one quality with it, so that I could be as much at home and citizen in it as where I actually lived. There I found joy and sorrow mixed, and nothing abstract or typical, but everything standing for itself, and not for some other thing. Then, I suppose it was the interfusion of humor through so much of it, that made it all precious and friendly. I think I had a native love of laughing, which was fostered in me by my father's way of looking at life, and had certainly been flattered by my intimacy with Cervantes; but whether this was so or not, I know that I liked best and felt deepest those plays and passages in Shakespeare where the alliance of the tragic and the comic was closest. Perhaps in a time when self-consciousness is so widespread, it is the only thing that saves us from ourselves. I am sure that without it I should not have been naturalized to that world of Shakespeare's Histories, where I used to

spend so much of my leisure, with such a sense of
his own intimate companionship there as I had no-
where else. I felt that he most somehow like my being in the joke of it all, and that in his great heart he
had room for a boy willing absolutely to lose himself
in him, and be as one of his creations.

It was the time of life with me when a boy begins
to be in love with the pretty faces that then peopled
this world so thickly, and I did not fail to fall in love
with the ladies of that Shakespeare-world where I
lived equally. I cannot tell whether it was because I
found them like my ideals here, or whether my ideals
acquired merit because of their likeness to the realities
there; they appeared to be all of one degree of enchanting loveliness; but upon the whole I must have
preferred them in the plays, because it was so much
easier to get on with them there; I was always much
better dressed there; I was vastly handsomer; I was
not bashful or afraid, and I had some defects of these
advantages to contend with here.

That friend of mine, the printer whom I have men-
tioned, was one with me in a sense of the Shakespearean humor, and he dwelt with me in the sort of
double being I had in those two worlds. We took the
book into the woods at the ends of the long summer

afternoons that remained to us when we had finished our work, and on the shining Sundays of the warm, late spring, the early, warm autumn, and we read it there on grassy slopes or heaps of fallen leaves; so that much of the poetry is mixed for me with a rapturous sense of the out-door beauty of this lovely natural world. We read turn about, one taking the story up as the other tired, and as we read the drama played itself under the open sky and in the free air with such orchestral effects as the soughing woods, or some rippling stream afforded. It was not interrupted when a squirrel dropped a nut on us from the top of a tall hickory; and the plaint of a meadow-lark prolonged itself with unbroken sweetness from one world to the other.

But I think it takes two to read in the open air. The pressure of walls is wanted to keep the mind within itself when one reads alone; otherwise it wanders and disperses itself through nature. When my friend left us for want of work in the office, or from the vagarious impulse which is so strong in our craft, I took my Shakespeare no longer to the woods and fields, but pored upon him mostly by night, in the narrow little space which I had for my study, under the stairs at home. There was a desk pushed back against the wall, which the irregular ceiling sloped down to meet behind it, and at my left was a window, which gave a good light on the writing-leaf of my desk. This was my workshop for six or seven years, and it was not at all a bad one; I have had many since that were not so much to the purpose; and though I would not live my life over, I would willingly enough have that little study mine again. But it is gone as utterly as the faces and voices that made home around it, and that I was fierce to shut out of it, so that no sound or sight should molest me in the pursuit of the end which I sought gropingly, blindly, with very little hope, but with an intense ambition, and a courage that gave way under no burden, before no obstacle. Long ago changes were made in the low, rambling house which threw my little closet into a larger room; but this was not until after I had left it many years; and as long as I remained a part of that dear and simple home it was my place to read, to write, to muse, to dream.

I sometimes wish in these later years that I had spent less time in it, or that world of books which it opened into ; that I had seen more of the actual world, and had learned to know my brethren in it better. I might so have amassed more material for after use in literature, but I had to fit myself to use it, and I suppose that this was what I was doing, in my own way, and by such light as I had. I often toiled wrongly and foolishly ; but certainly I toiled, and I suppose no work is wasted. Some strength I hope was coming to me, even from my mistakes, and though I went over ground that I need not have traversed, if I had not been left so much to find the way alone, yet I was not standing still, and some of the things that I then wished to do I have done. I do not mind owning that in others I have failed. For instance, I have never surpassed Shakespeare as a poet, though I once firmly meant to do so ; but then, it is to be remembered that very few other people have surpassed him, and that it would not have been easy.

XIV.

IK MARVEL.

My ardor for Shakespeare must have been at its height when I was between sixteen and seventeen years old, for I fancy when I began to formulate my admiration, and to try to measure his greatness in phrases, I was less simply impassioned than at some earlier time. At any rate, I am sure that I did not proclaim his planetary importance in creation until I was at least nineteen. But even at an earlier age I no longer worshiped at a single shrine; there were many gods in the temple of my idolatry, and I bowed the knee to them all in a devotion which, if it was not of one quality, was certainly impartial. While I was reading, and thinking, and living Shakespeare with such an intensity that I do not see how there could have been room in my consciousness for anything else, there seem to have been half a dozen other divinities there, great and small, whom I have some present difficulty in distinguishing. I kept Irving, and Goldsmith, and Cervantes on their old altars, but I added new ones, and these I translated from the contemporary literary world quite as often as from the past. I am rather glad that among them was the gentle and kindly Ik Marvel, whose Reveries of a Bachelor and whose Dream Life the young people of that day were reading with a tender rapture which will not be altogether surprising, I dare say, to the young people of this. The books have survived the span of immortality fixed by our amusing copyright laws, and seem now, when any pirate publisher may plunder their author, to have a new life before them. Perhaps this is ordered by Providence, that those who have no right to them may profit by them, in that divine contempt of such profit which Providence so often shows.

I cannot understand just how I came to know of the books, but I suppose it was through the contemporary criticism which I was then beginning to read, wherever I could find it, in the magazines and newspapers; and I could not say just why I thought it would be very *comme il faut* to like them. Probably the literary fine world, which is always rubbing shoulders with the other fine world, and bringing off a little of its powder and perfume, was then dawning upon me, and I was wishing to be of it, and to like the things that it liked; I am not so anxious to do it now. But if this is true, I found the books better than their friends, and had many a heartache from their pathos, many a genuine glow of purpose from their high import, many a tender suffusion from their sentiment. I dare say I should find their pose now a little old-fashioned. I believe it was rather full of sighs, and shrugs, and starts, expressed in dashes, and asterisks, and exclamations, but I am sure that the feeling was the genuine and manly sort which is of all times and always the latest wear. Whatever it was, it sufficed to win my heart, and to identify me with whatever was most romantic and most pathetic in it. I read Dream Life first—though the Reveries of a Bachelor was written first, and I believe is esteemed the better book—and Dream Life remains first in my affections. I have now little notion what it was about, but I love its memory. The book is associated especially in my mind with one golden day of Indian summer, when I carried it into the woods with me, and abandoned myself to a welter of emotion over its page. I lay under a crimson maple, and I remember how the light struck through it and flushed the print with the gules of the foliage. My friend was away by this time on one of his several absences in the Northwest, and I was quite alone in the absurd and irrelevant melancholy with which I read myself and my circumstances into the book. I began to read them out again in due time, clothed with the literary airs and graces that I admired in it, and for a long time I imitated Ik Marvel in the voluminous letters I wrote my friend in compliance with his Shakespearean prayer:

> "To Milan let me hear from thee by letters,
> Of thy success in love, and what news else
> Betideth here in absence of thy friend;
> And I likewise will visit thee with mine."

Milan was then presently Sheboygan, Wisconsin, and Verona was our little village; but they both served the soul of youth as well as the real places would have done, and were as really Italian as anything else in the situation was really this or that. Heaven knows what gaudy sentimental parade we made in our borrowed plumes, but if the travesty had kept itself to the written word it would have been all well enough. My misfortune was to carry it into print when I began to write a story in the Ik Marvel manner, or rather to compose it in type at the case, for that was what I did; and it was not altogether imitated from Ik Marvel either, for I drew upon the easier art of Dickens at times, and helped myself out with bald parodies of Bleak House in many places. It was all very well at the beginning, but I had not reckoned with the future sufficiently to have started with any clear ending in my mind, and as I went on I began to find myself more and more in doubt about it. My material gave out; incidents failed me; the characters wavered and threatened to perish on my hands. To crown my misery there grew up an impatience with the story among its readers, and this found its way to me one day when I overheard an old farmer who came in for his paper say that he did not think that story amounted to much. I did not think so either, but it was deadly to have it put into words, and how I escaped the mortal effect of the stroke I do not know. Somehow I managed to bring the wretched thing to a close, and to live it slowly into the past. Slowly it seemed then, but I dare say it was fast enough; and there is always this consolation to be whispered in the ear of wounded vanity, that the world's memory is equally bad for failure and success; that if it will not keep your triumphs in mind as you think it ought, neither will it long dwell upon your defeats. But that experience was really terrible. It was like some dreadful dream one has of finding one's self in battle without the courage needed to carry one creditably through the action, or on the stage unprepared by study of the part which one is to appear in. I have never looked at that story since, so great was the shame and anguish that I suffered from it, and yet I do not think it was badly conceived, or attempted upon lines that were false or wrong. If it were not for what happened in the past I might like some time to write a story on the same lines in the future.

XV.

DICKENS.

What I have said of Dickens reminds me that I had been reading him at the same time that I had been reading Ik Marvel; but a curious thing about the reading of my later boyhood is that the dates do not sharply detach themselves one from another. This may be so because my reading was much more multifarious than it had been earlier, or because I was reading always two or three authors at a time. I think Macaulay a little antedated Dickens in my affections, but when I came to the novels of that masterful artist (as I must call him, with a thousand reservations as to the times when he is not a master and not an artist), I did not fail to fall under his spell.

This was in a season of great depression, when I began to feel in broken health the effect of trying to burn my candle at both ends. It seemed for a while very simple and easy to come home in the middle of the afternoon, when my task at the printing-office was done, and sit down to my books in my little study, which I did not finally leave until the family were in bed; but it was not well, and it was not enough that I should like to do it. The most that can be said in defense of such a thing is that with the strong native impulse and the conditions it was inevitable. If I was to do the thing I wanted to do I was to do it in that way, and I wanted to do that thing, whatever it was, more than I wanted to do anything else, and even more than I wanted to do nothing. I cannot make out that I was fond of study, or cared for the things I was trying to do, except as a means to other things. As far as my pleasure went, or my natural bent was concerned, I would rather have been wandering through the woods with a gun on my shoulder, or lying under a tree, or reading some book that cost me no sort of effort. But there was much more than my pleasure involved; there was a hope to fulfill, an aim to achieve, and I could no more have left off trying for what I hoped and aimed at than I could have left off living, though I did not know very distinctly what either was. As I look back at the endeavor of those days much of it seems mere purblind groping, willful and wandering. I can see that doing all by myself I was not truly a law to myself, but only a sort of helpless force.

I studied Latin because I believed that I should read the Latin authors, and I suppose I got as much of the language as most school-boys of my age, but I never read any Latin author but Cornelius Nepos. I studied Greek, and I learned so much of it as to read a chapter of the Testament, and an ode of Anacreon. Then I left it, not because I did not mean to go farther, or indeed stop short of reading all Greek literature, but because that friend of mine and I talked it over and decided that I could go on with Greek any time, but I had better for the present study German, with the help of a German who had come to the village. Apparently I was carrying forward an attack on French at the same time, for I distinctly recall my failure to enlist with me an old gentleman who had once lived a long time in France, and whom I hoped to get at least an accent from. Perhaps because he knew he had no accent worth speaking of, or perhaps because he did not want the bother of imparting it, he never would keep any of the engagements he made with me, and when we did meet he so abounded in excuses and subterfuges that he finally escaped me, and I was left to acquire an Italian accent of French in Venice seven or eight years later. At the same time I was reading Spanish, more or less, but neither wisely nor too well. Having had so little help in my studies, I had a stupid pride in refusing all, even such as I might have availed myself of, without shame, in books, and I would not read any Spanish author with English notes. I would have him in an edition wholly Spanish from beginning to end, and I would fight my way through him single-handed, with only such aid as I must borrow from a lexicon.

I now call this stupid, but I have really no more right to blame the boy who was once I than I have to praise him, and I am certainly not going to do that. In his day and place he did what he could in his own way; he had no true perspective of life, but I do not know that youth ever has that. Some strength came to him finally from the mere struggle, undirected and misdirected as it often was, and such mental fibre as he had was toughened by the prolonged stress. It could be said, of course, that the time apparently wasted in these effectless studies could have been well spent in deepening and widening a knowledge of English literature never yet too great, and I have often

said this myself; but then, again, I am not sure that
the studies were altogether effectless.   I have sometimes thought that greater skill had come to my hand
from them than it would have had without, and I have
trusted that in making known to me the sources of so
much English, my little Latin and less Greek have
enabled me to use my own speech with a subtler sense
of it than I should have had otherwise.

But I will by no means insist upon my conjecture.
What is certain is that for the present my studies,
without method and without stint, began to tell upon
my health, and that my nerves gave way in all manner
of hypochondriacal fears.   These finally resolved themselves into one, incessant, inexorable, which I could
escape only through bodily fatigue, or through some
absorbing interest that took me out of myself altogether and filled my morbid mind with the images of
another's creation.

In this mood I first read Dickens, whom I had
known before in the reading I had listened to.   But
now I devoured his books one after another as fast as
I could read them.   I plunged from the heart of one
to another, so as to leave myself no chance for the
horrors that beset me.   Some of them remain associated with the gloom and misery of that time, so that

when I take them up they bring back its dreadful shadow. But I have since read them all more than once, and I have had my time of thinking Dickens, talking Dickens, and writing Dickens, as we all had who lived in the days of the mighty magician. I fancy the readers who have come to him since he ceased to fill the world with his influence can have little notion how great it was. In that time he colored the parlance of the English-speaking race, and formed upon himself every minor talent attempting fiction. While his glamour lasted it was no more possible for a young novelist to escape writing Dickens than it was for a young poet to escape writing Tennyson. I admired other authors more; I loved them more, but when it came to a question of trying to do something in fiction I was compelled, as by a law of nature, to do it at least partially in his way.

All the while that he held me so fast by his potent charm I was aware that it was a very rough magic, now and again, but I could not assert my sense of this against him in matters of character and structure. To these I gave in helplessly; their very grotesqueness was proof of their divine origin, and I bowed to the crudest manifestations of his genius in these kinds as if they were revelations not to be doubted without sacrilege. But in certain small matters, as it were of ritual, I suffered myself to think, and I remember boldly speaking my mind about his style, which I thought bad.

I spoke it even to the quaint character whom I borrowed his books from, and who might almost have come out of his books. He lived in Dickens in a measure that I have never known another to do, and my contumely must have brought him a pang that was truly a personal grief. He forgave it, no doubt because I bowed in the Dickens worship without question on all other points. He was then a man well on toward fifty, and he had come to America early in life, and had lived in our village many years, without casting one of his English prejudices, or ceasing to be of a contrary opinion on every question, political, religious and social. He had no fixed belief, but he went to the service of his church whenever it was held among us, and he revered the Book of Common Prayer while he disputed the authority of the Bible with all comers. He had become a citizen, but he despised democracy, and achieved a hardy consistency only by voting with the pro-slavery party upon all measures friendly to the institution which he considered the scandal and reproach of the American name. From a heart tender to all, he liked to say wanton, savage and cynical things, but he bore no malice if you gainsaid him. I know nothing of his origin, except the fact of his being an Englishman, or what his first calling had been; but he had evolved among us from a house-painter to an organ-builder, and he had a passionate love of music. He built his organs from the ground up, and made every part of them with his own hands; I believe they were very good, and at any rate the churches in the country about took them from him as fast as he could make them. He had one in his own house, and it was fine to see him as he sat before it, with his long, tremulous hands outstretched to the keys, his noble head thrown back and his sensitive face lifted in the rapture of his music. He was a rarely intelligent creature, and an artist in every fibre; and if you did not quarrel with his manifold perversities, he was a delightful companion.

After my friend went away I fell much to him for society, and we took long, rambling walks together, or sat on the stoop before his door, or lounged over the books in the drug-store, and talked evermore of literature. He must have been nearly three times my age, but that did not matter; we met in the equality of the ideal world where there is neither old nor young, any more than there is rich or poor. He had read a great deal, but of all he had read he liked Dickens best, and was always coming back to him with affection, whenever the talk strayed. He could not make me out when I criticized the style of Dickens; and when I praised Thackeray's style to the disadvantage of Dickens's he could only accuse me of a sort of æsthetic snobbishness in my preference. Dickens, he said, was for the million, and Thackeray was for the upper ten thousand. His view amused me at the time, and yet I am not sure that it was altogether mistaken.

There is certainly a property in Thackeray that somehow flatters the reader into the belief that he is better than other people; and with a young man especially he is of an insidiously aristocratic effect. I do not mean to say that this was why I thought him a finer writer than Dickens, but I will own that it was probably one of the reasons why I liked him better; if I appreciated him so fully as I felt, I must be of a finer porcelain than the earthen pots which were not aware of any particular difference in the various liquors poured into them. In Dickens the virtue of his social defect is that he never appeals to the principle which sniffs, in his reader. The base of his work is the whole breadth and depth of humanity itself. It is helplessly elemental, but it is not the less grandly so, and if it deals with the simpler manifestations of character, character affected by the interests and passions rather than the tastes and preferences, it certainly deals with the larger moods through them. I do not know that in the whole range of his work he once suffers us to feel our superiority to a fellow-creature through any social accident, or except for some moral cause. This makes him very fit reading for a boy, and I should say that a boy could get only good from him. His view of the world and of society, though it was very little philosophized, was instinctively sane and reasonable, even when it was most impossible.

We are just beginning to discern that certain conceptions of our relations to our fellow-men, once formulated in generalities which met with a dramatic acceptation from the world, and were then rejected by it as mere rhetoric, have really a vital truth in them, and that if they have ever seemed false it was because of the false conditions in which we still live. Equality and fraternity, these are the ideals which once moved the world, and then fell into despite and mockery, as unrealities; but now they assert themselves in our hearts once more.

Blindly, unwittingly, erringly as Dickens often

urged them, these ideals mark the whole tendency of
his fiction, and they are what endear him to the heart,
and will keep him dear to it long after many a cun-
ninger artificer in letters has passed into forgetfulness.
I do not pretend that I perceived the full scope of his
books, but I was aware of it in the finer sense which
is not consciousness. While I read him, I was in a
world where the right came out best, as I believe it
will yet do in this world, and where merit was crowned
with the success which I believe will yet attend it in
our daily life, untrammeled by social convention or
economic circumstance. In that world of his, in the
ideal world, to which the real world must finally conform itself, I dwelt among the shows of things, but
under a Providence that governed all things to a good
end, and where neither wealth nor birth could avail
against virtue or right. Of course it was in a way all
crude enough, and was already contradicted by experience in the small sphere of my own being; but never-
theless it was true with that truth which is at the
bottom of things, and I was happy in it. I could not
fail to love the mind which conceived it, and my worship of Dickens was more grateful than that I had yet
given any writer. I did not establish with him that
one-sided understanding which I had with Cervantes

and Shakespeare; with a contemporary that was not possible, and as an American I was deeply hurt at the things he had said against us, and the more hurt because I felt that they were often so just. But I was for the time entirely his, and I could not have wished to write like any one else.

I do not pretend that the spell I was under was wholly of a moral or social texture. For the most part I was charmed with him because he was a delightful story teller; because he could thrill me, and make me hot and cold; because he could make me laugh and cry, and stop my pulse and breath at will. There seemed an inexhaustible source of humor and pathos in his work, which I now find choked and dry; I cannot laugh any more at Pickwick or Sam Weller, or weep for little Nell or Paul Dombey; their jokes, their griefs, seemed to me to be turned on, and to have a mechanical action. But beneath all is still the strong drift of a genuine emotion, a sympathy, deep and sincere, with the poor, the lowly, the unfortunate. In all that vast range of fiction, there is nothing that tells for the strong, because they are strong, against the weak, nothing that tells for the haughty against the humble, nothing that tells for wealth against poverty. The effect of Dickens is purely democratic, and however contemptible he found our pseudo-equality, he was more truly democratic than any American who had yet written fiction. I suppose it was our instinctive perception in the region of his instinctive expression, that made him so dear to us, and wounded our silly vanity so keenly through our love when he told us the truth about our horrible sham of a slave-based freedom. But at any rate the democracy is there in his work more than he knew perhaps, or would ever have known, or ever recognized by his own life. In fact, when one comes to read the story of his life, and to know that he was really and lastingly ashamed of having once put up shoe-blacking as a boy, and was unable to forgive his mother for suffering him to be so degraded, one perceives that he too was the slave of conventions and the victim of conditions which it is the highest function of his fiction to help destroy.

I imagine that my early likes and dislikes in Dickens were not very discriminating. I liked David Copperfield, and Barnaby Rudge, and Bleak House, and I still like them; but I do not think I liked them more than Dombey & Son, and Nicholas Nickleby, and the Pickwick Papers, which I cannot read now with any sort of patience, not to speak of pleasure. I liked Martin Chuzzlewit, too, and the other day I read a great part of it again, and found it roughly true in the passages that referred to America, though it was surcharged in the serious moods, and caricatured in the comic. The English are always inadequate observers; they seem too full of themselves to have eyes and ears for any alien people; but as far as an Englishman could, Dickens had caught the look of our life in certain aspects. His report of it was clumsy and farcical; it wanted nicety of accent and movement, but in a large, loose way it was like enough; at least he had caught the note of our self-satisfied, intolerant and hypocritical provinciality, and this was not altogether lost in his mocking horse-play.

I cannot make out that I was any the less fond of Dickens because of it. I believe I was rather more willing to accept it as a faithful portraiture then than I should be now; and I certainly never made any question of it with my friend the organ-builder. Martin Chuzzlewit was a favorite book with him, and so was the Old Curiosity Shop. No doubt a fancied affinity with Tom Pinch through their common love of music made him like that most sentimental and improbable personage, whom he would have disowned and laughed to scorn if he had met him in life; but it was a purely altruistic sympathy that he felt with

Little Nell and her grandfather. He was fond of reading the pathetic passages from both books, and I can still hear his rich, vibrant voice as it lingered in tremulous emotion on the periods he loved. He would catch the volume up anywhere, any time, and begin to read, at the book-store, or the harness-shop, or the law-office, it did not matter in the wide leisure of a country village, in those days before the war, when people had all the time there was; and he was sure of his audience as long as he chose to read. One Christmas eve, in answer to a general wish, he read the Christmas Carol in the Court House, and people came from all about to hear him.

He was an invalid and he died long since, ending a life of suffering in the saddest way. Several years before his death money fell to his family, and he went with them to an Eastern city, where he tried in vain to make himself at home. He never ceased to pine for the village he had left, with its old companionships, its easy usages, its familiar faces; and he escaped to it again and again, till at last every tie was severed, and he could come back no more. He was never reconciled to the change, and in a manner he did really die of the homesickness which deepened an hereditary taint, and enfeebled him to the disorder that carried him off. My memories of Dickens remain mingled with my memories of this quaint and most original genius, and though I knew Dickens long before I knew his lover, I can scarcely think of one without thinking of the other.

XVI.

WORDSWORTH, LOWELL, CHAUCER.

CERTAIN other books I associate with another pathetic nature, of whom the organ-builder and I were both fond. This was the young poet who looked after the book half of the village drug and book store, and who wrote poetry in such leisure as he found from his duties, and with such strength as he found in the disease preying upon him. He must have been far gone in consumption when I first knew him, for I have no recollection of a time when his voice was not faint and husky, his sweet smile wan, and his blue eyes dull with the disease that wasted him away,

> " Like wax in the fire,
> Like snow in the sun."

People spoke of him as once strong and vigorous, but I recall him fragile and pale, gentle, patient, knowing his inexorable doom, and not hoping or seeking to es-

cape it. As the end drew near he left his employment
and went home to the farm, some twenty miles away,
where I drove out to see him once in the depths of a
winter which was to be his last. My heart was heavy
all the time, but he tried to make the visit pass cheer-
fully with our wonted talk about books. Only at
parting, when he took my hand in his thin, cold
clasp, he said, " I suppose my disease is progressing,"
with the same patience that he always showed.

I did not see him again, and I am not sure now
that his gift was very distinct or very great. It was
slight and graceful rather, I fancy, and if he had lived
it might not have sufficed to make him widely known,
but he had a real and a very delicate sense of beauty
in literature, and I believe it was through sympathy
with his preferences that I came into appreciation of
several authors whom I had not known, or had not
cared for before. There could not have been many
shelves of books in that store, and I came to be pretty
well acquainted with them all before I began to buy
them. For the most part, I do not think it occurred
to me that they were there to be sold; for this pale
poet seemed indifferent to the commercial property in
them, and seemed only to wish me to like them.

I am not sure, but I think it was through some volumes which I found in his charge that I first came to know of De Quincey; he was fond of Dr. Holmes's poetry; he loved Whittier and Longfellow, each represented in his slender stock by some distinctive work. There were several stray volumes of Thackeray's minor writings, and I still have the Yellowplush Papers in the smooth red cloth (now pretty well tattered) of Appleton's Popular Library, which I bought there. But most of the books were in the famous old brown cloth of Ticknor & Fields, which was a warrant of excellence in the literature it covered. Besides these there were standard volumes of poetry, published by Phillips & Sampson, from worn-out plates; for a birthday present my mother got me Wordsworth in this shape, and I am glad to think that I once read the Excursion in it, for I do not think I could do so now, and I have a feeling that it is very right and fit to have read the Excursion. To be honest, it was very hard reading even then, and I could not truthfully pretend that I have ever liked Wordsworth except in parts, though for the matter of that, I do not suppose that any one ever did. I tried hard enough to like everything in him, for I had already learned enough to know that I ought to like him, and that if I did not, it was a proof of intellectual and moral inferiority

in me.   My early idol, Pope, had already been tum-
bled into the dust by Lowell, whose lectures on English Poetry had lately been given in Boston, and had
met with my rapturous acceptance in such newspaper
report as I had got of them.   So, my preoccupations
were all in favor of the Lake School, and it was both
in my will and my conscience to like Wordsworth.   If
I did not do so it was not my fault, and the fault remains very much what it first was.

I feel and understand him more deeply than I did
then, but I do not think that I then failed of the
meaning of much that I read in him, and I am sure
that my senses were quick to all the beauty in him.
After suffering once through the Excursion I did not
afflict myself with it again, but there were other poems
of his which I read over and over, as I fancy it is the
habit of every lover of poetry to do with the pieces he
is fond of.   Still, I do not make out that Wordsworth
was ever a passion of mine ; on the other hand, neither
was Byron.   Him, too, I liked in passages and in certain poems before I read Wordsworth at all; I read
him throughout, but I did not try to imitate him, and
I did not try to imitate Wordsworth.

Those lectures of Lowell's had a great influence
with me, and I tried to like whatever they bade me

like, after a fashion common to all young people when
they begin to read criticisms; their æsthetic pride is
touched; they wish to realize that they too can feel
the fine things the critic admires. From this motive
they do a great deal of factitious liking; but after all
the affections will not be bidden, and the critic can
only avail to give a point of view, to enlighten a perspective. When I read Lowell's praises of him, I had
all the will in the world to read Spencer, and I really
meant to do so, but I have not done so to this day,
and as often as I have tried I have found it impossible. It was not so with Chaucer, whom I loved from
the first word of his which I found quoted in those
lectures, and in Chambers's Encyclopædia of English
Literature, which I had borrowed of my friend the
organ-builder.

In fact, I may fairly class Chaucer among my passions, for I read him with that sort of personal attach-
ment I had for Cervantes, who resembled him in a
certain sweet and cheery humanity. But I do not
allege this as the reason, for I had the same feeling
for Pope, who was not like either of them. Kissing
goes by favor, in literature as in life, and one cannot
quite account for one's passions in either; what is certain is, I liked Chaucer and I did not like Spencer;

possibly there was an affinity between reader and poet, but if there was I should be at a loss to name it, unless it was the liking for reality, and the sense of mother earth in human life. By the time I had read all of Chaucer that I could find in the various collections and criticisms, my father had been made a clerk in the legislature, and on one of his visits home he brought me the poet's works from the State Library, and I set about reading them with a glossary. It was not easy, but it brought strength with it, and lifted my heart with a sense of noble companionship.

I will not pretend that I was insensible to the grossness of the poet's time, which I found often enough in the poet's verse, as well as the goodness of his nature, and my father seems to have felt a certain misgiving about it. He repeated to me the librarian's question as to whether he thought he ought to put an unexpurgated edition in the hands of a boy, and his own answer that he did not believe it would hurt me. It was a kind of appeal to me to make the event justify him, and I suppose he had not given me the book without due reflection. Probably he reasoned that with my greed for all manner of literature the bad would become known to me along with the good at any rate, and I had better know that he knew it.

The streams of filth flow down through the ages in literature, which sometimes seems little better than an open sewer, and, as I have said, I do not see why the time should not come when the noxious and noisome channels should be stopped; but the base of the mind is bestial, and so far the beast in us has insisted upon having his full say. The worst of lewd literature is that it seems to give a sanction to lewdness in the life, and that inexperience takes this effect for reality: that is the danger and the harm, and I think the fact ought not to be blinked. Compared with the meaner poets the greater are the cleaner, and Chaucer was probably safer than any other English poet of his time, but I am not going to pretend that there are not things in Chaucer which one would be the better for not reading; and so far as these words of mine shall be taken for counsel, I am not willing that they should unqualifiedly praise him. The matter is by no means simple; it is not easy to conceive of a means of purifying the literature of the past without weakening it, and even falsifying it, but it is best to own that it is in all respects just what it is, and not to feign it otherwise. I am not ready to say that the harm from it is positive, but you do get smeared with it, and the filthy thought lives with the filthy rhyme in the ear,

even when it does not corrupt the heart or make it
seem a light thing for the reader's tongue and pen to
sin in kind.

I loved my Chaucer too well, I hope, not to get
some good from the best in him; and my reading of
criticism had taught me how and where to look for the
best, and to know it when I had found it. Of course
I began to copy him. That is, I did not attempt anything like his tales in kind; they must have seemed
too hopelessly far away in taste and time, but I studied his verse, and imitated a stanza which I found in
some of his things and had not found elsewhere; I rejoiced in the freshness and sweetness of his diction,
and though I felt that his structure was obsolete, there
was in his wording something homelier and heartier
than the imported analogues that had taken the place
of the phrases he used.

I began to employ in my own work the archaic
words that I fancied most, which was futile and foolish
enough, and I formed a preference for the simpler
Anglo-Saxon woof of our speech, which was not so
bad. Of course, being left so much as I was to my
own whim and caprice in such things, I could not keep
a just mean; I had an aversion for the Latin deriva-
tives which was nothing short of a craze. Some half-

bred critic whom I had read made me believe that
English could be written without them, and had better
be written so, and I did not escape from this lament-
able error until I had produced with weariness and vex-
ation of spirit several pieces of prose wholly composed
of monosyllables. I suspect now that I did not always
stop to consider whether my short words were not as
Latin by race as any of the long words I rejected, and
that I only made sure they were short.

The frivolous ingenuity which wasted itself in this
exercise happily could not hold out long, and in verse
it was pretty well helpless from the beginning. Yet
I will not altogether blame it, for it made me know,
as nothing else could, the resources of our tongue in
that sort; and in the revolt from the slavish bondage
I took upon myself I did not go so far as to plunge
into any very wild polysyllabic excesses. I still like
the little word if it says the thing I want to say as
well as the big one, but I honor above all the word
that says the thing. At the same time I confess that
I have a prejudice against certain words that I cannot overcome; the sight of some offends me, the sound
of others, and rather than use one of those detested vo-
cables, even when I perceive that it would convey
my exact meaning, I would cast about long for some

other. I think this is a foible, and a disadvantage, but I do not deny it.

An author who had much to do with preparing me for the quixotic folly in point was that good Thomas Babington Macaulay, who taught simplicity of diction in phrases of as "learned length and thundering sound," as any he would have had me shun, and who deplored the Latinistic English of Johnson in terms emulous of the great doctor's orotundity and ponderosity. I wonder now that I did not see how my physician avoided his medicine, but I did not, and I went on to spend myself in an endeavor as vain and senseless as any that pedantry has conceived. It was none the less absurd because I believed in it so devoutly, and sacrificed myself to it with such infinite pains and labor. But this was long after I read Macaulay, who was one of my grand passions before Dickens or Chaucer.

XVII.

MACAULAY.

ONE of the many characters of the village was the machinist who had his shop under our printing-office when we first brought our newspaper to the place, and who was just then a machinist because he was tired of being many other things, and had not yet made up his mind what he should be next. He could have been whatever he turned his agile intellect and his cunning hand to; he had been a schoolmaster and a watchmaker, and I believe an amateur doctor and irregular lawyer; he talked and wrote brilliantly, and he was one of the group that nightly disposed of every manner of theoretical and practical question at the drug-store; it was quite indifferent to him which side he took; what he enjoyed was the mental exercise. He was in consumption, as so many were in that region, and he carbonized against it, as he said; he took his carbon in the liquid form, and the last time I saw him the carbon had finally prevailed over the consumption, but it had itself become a seated vice; that was many years since, and it is many years since he died.

He must have been known to me earlier, but I remember him first as he swam vividly into my ken, with a volume of Macaulay's essays in his hand, one day. Less figuratively speaking, he came up into the printing-office to expose from the book the nefarious plagiarism of an editor in a neighboring city, who had adapted with the change of names and a word or two here and there, whole passages from the essay on Barère, to the denunciation of a brother editor. It was a very simple-hearted fraud, and it was all done with an innocent trust in the popular ignorance which now seems to me a little pathetic; but it was certainly very bare-faced, and merited the public punishment which the discoverer inflicted by means of what journalists call the deadly parallel column. The effect ought logically to have been ruinous for the plagiarist, but it was really nothing of the kind. He simply ignored the exposure, and the comments of the other city papers, and in the process of time he easily lived down the memory of it and went on to greater usefulness in his profession.

But for the moment it appeared to me a tremendous crisis, and I listened as the minister of justice read his communication, with a thrill which lost itself in the interest I suddenly felt in the plundered author. Those facile, and shallow, and brilliant phrases and ideas struck me as the finest things I had yet known in literature, and I borrowed the book and read it through. Then I borrowed another volume of Macaulay's essays, and another and another, till I had read them every one. It was like a long debauch, from which I emerged with regret that it should ever end.

I tried other essayists, other critics, whom the machinist had in his library, but it was useless; neither Sidney Smith nor Thomas Carlyle could console me; I sighed for more Macaulay and evermore Macaulay. I read his history of England, and I could measurably console myself with that, but only measurably; and I could not go back to the essays and read them again, for it seemed to me I had absorbed them so thoroughly that I had left nothing unenjoyed in them. I used to talk with the machinist about them, and with the organ-builder, and with my friend the printer, but no one seemed to feel the intense fascination for them that I did, and that I should now be quite unable to account for.

Once more I had an author for whom I could feel
a personal devotion, whom I could dream of and dote
upon, and whom I could offer my intimacy in many
an impassioned revery. I do not think T. B. Macaulay would really have liked it; I dare say he would
not have valued the friendship of the sort of a youth
I was, but in the conditions he was helpless, and I
poured out my love upon him without a rebuff. Of
course I reformed my prose style, which had been
carefully modeled upon that of Goldsmith and Irving,
and began to write in the manner of Macaulay, in
short, quick sentences, and with the prevalent use of
brief Anglo-Saxon words, which he prescribed, but
did not practice. As for his notions of literature, I
simply accepted them with the feeling that any question of them would have been little better than
blasphemy.

For a long time he spoiled my taste for any other
criticism; he made it seem pale, and poor and weak;
and he blunted my sense to subtler excellences than I
found in him. I think this was a pity, but it was a
thing not to be helped, like a great many things that
happen to our hurt in life; it was simply inevitable.
How or when my frenzy for him began to abate I
cannot say, but it certainly waned, and it must have

waned rapidly, for after no great while I found myself feeling the charm of quite different minds, as
fully as if his had never enslaved me. I cannot regret
that I enjoyed him so keenly as I did; it was in a
way a generous delight, and though he swayed me
helplessly whatever way he thought, I do not think
yet that he swayed me in any very wrong way.   He
was a bright and clear intelligence, and if his light
did not go far, it is to be said of him that his worst
fault was only to have stopped short of the finest
truth in art, in morals, in politics.

XVIII.

CRITICS AND REVIEWS.

WHAT remained to me from my love of Macaulay was a love of reading criticism, and I read almost as much in criticism as I read in poetry and history and fiction. It was of an eccentric doctor, another of the village characters, that I got the works of Edgar A. Poe; I do not know just how, but it must have been in some exchange of books; he preferred metaphysics. At any rate I fell greedily upon them, and I read with no less zest than his poems the bitter, and cruel, and narrow-minded criticisms which mainly filled one of the volumes. As usual, I accepted them implicitly, and it was not till long afterward that I understood how worthless they were.

I think that hardly less immoral than the lubricity of literature, and its celebration of the monkey and the goat in us, is the spectacle it affords of the tiger-

ish play of satire. It is monstrous that for no offense
but the wish to produce something beautiful, and the
mistake of his powers in that direction, a writer
should become the prey of some ferocious wit, and
that his tormentor should achieve credit by his light-
ness and ease in rending his prey ; it is shocking to
think how alluring and depraving the fact is to the
young reader emulous of such credit, and eager to
achieve it.   Because I admired these barbarities of
Poe's, I wished to imitate them, to impale some hapless victim on my own spear, to make him suffer and
to make the reader laugh.   This is as far as possible
from the criticism that enlightens and ennobles, but it
is still the ideal of most critics, deny it as they will;
and because it is the ideal of most critics criticism
still remains behind all the other literary arts.

I am glad to remember that at the same time I
exulted in these ferocities I had mind enough and
heart enough to find pleasure in the truer and finer
work, the humaner work of other writers, like Hazlitt,
and Leigh Hunt and Lamb, which became known to
me at a date I cannot exactly fix.   I believe it was
Hazlitt.whom I read first, and he helped me to clarify
and formulate my admiration of Shakespeare as no
one else had yet done; Lamb helped me too, and with

all the dramatists, and on every hand I was reaching out for light that should enable me to place in literary history the authors I knew and loved.

I fancy it was well for me at this period to have got at the four great English reviews, the Edinburgh, the Westminster, the London Quarterly and the North British, which I read regularly, as well as Blackwood's Magazine. We got them in the American editions in payment for printing the publisher's prospectus, and their arrival was an excitement, a joy and a satisfaction with me, which I could not now describe without having to accuse myself of exaggeration. The love of literature, and the hope of doing something in it, had become my life to the exclusion of all other interests, or it was at least the great reality, and all other things were as shadows. I was living in a time of high political tumult, and I certainly cared very much for the question of slavery which was then filling the minds of men; I felt deeply the shame and wrong of our Fugitive Slave Law; I was stirred by the news from Kansas, where the great struggle between the two great principles in our nationality was beginning in bloodshed; but I cannot pretend that any of these things were more than ripples on the surface of my intense and profound interest in literature. If I was not to live by it, I was somehow to live for it.

If I thought of taking up some other calling it was as a means only; literature was always the end I had in view, immediately or finally. I did not see how it was to yield me a living, for I knew that almost all the literary men in the country had other professions; they were editors, lawyers, or had public or private employments; or they were men of wealth; there was then not one who earned his bread solely by his pen in fiction, or drama, or history, or poetry, or criticism, in a day when people wanted very much less butter on their bread than they do now. But I kept blindly at my studies, and yet not altogether blindly, for, as I have said, the reading I did had more tendency than before, and I was beginning to see authors in their proportion to one another, and to the body of literature.

The English reviews were of great use to me in this; I made a rule of reading each one of them quite through. To be sure I often broke this rule, as people are apt to do with rules of the kind; it was not possible for a boy to wade through heavy articles relating to English politics and economics, but I do not think I left any paper upon a literary topic unread, and I did read enough politics, especially in Black-wood's, to be of Tory opinions; they were very fit opinions for a boy, and they did not exact of me any change in regard to the slavery question.

XIX.

A NON-LITERARY EPISODE.

I SUPPOSE I might almost class my devotion to
English reviews among my literary passions, but it
was of very short lease, not beyond a year or two at
the most. In the midst of it I made my first and only
essay aside from the lines of literature, or rather
wholly apart from it. After some talk with my father
it was decided, mainly by myself, I suspect, that I
should leave the printing-office and study law; and it
was arranged with the United States Senator who
lived in our village, and who was at home from Washington for the summer, that I was to come into his
office. The Senator was by no means to undertake
my instruction himself; his nephew, who had just begun to read law, was to be my fellow-student, and we
were to keep each other up to the work, and to recite
to each other, until we thought we had enough law to

go before a board of attorneys and test our fitness for admission to the bar.

This was the custom in that day and place, as I suppose it is still in most parts of the country. We were to be fitted for practice in the courts, not only by our reading, but by a season of pettifogging before justices of the peace, which I looked forward to with no small shrinking of my shy spirit; but what really troubled me most, and was always the grain of sand between my teeth, was Blackstone's confession of his own original preference for literature, and his perception that the law was "a jealous mistress," who would suffer no rival in his affections. I agreed with him that I could not go through life with a divided interest; I must give up literature or I must give up law. I not only consented to this logically, but I realized it in my attempt to carry on the reading I had loved, and to keep at the efforts I was always making to write something in verse or prose, at night, after studying law all day. The strain was great enough when I had merely the work in the printing-office; but now I came home from my Blackstone mentally fagged, and I could not take up the authors whom at the bottom of my heart I loved so much better. I tried it a month, but almost from the fatal day when I found that confession of Blackstone's, my whole being turned from the "jealous mistress" to the high-minded muses.

I had not only to go back to literature, but I had also to go back to the printing-office. I did not regret it, but I had made my change of front in the public eye, and I felt that it put me at a certain disadvantage with my fellow-citizens; as for the Senator, whose office I had forsaken, I met him now and then in the street, without trying to detain him, and once when he came to the printing-office for his paper we encountered at a point where we could not help speaking. He looked me over in my general effect of base mechanical, and asked me if I had given up the law; I had only to answer him I had, and our conference ended.

It was a terrible moment for me, because I knew that in his opinion I had chosen a path in life, which if it did not lead to the Poor House was at least no way to the White House. I suppose now that he thought I had merely gone back to my trade, and so for the time I had; but I have no reason to suppose that he judged my case narrow-mindedly, and I ought to have had the courage to have the affair out with him, and tell him just why I had left the law; we had

sometimes talked the English reviews over, for he read
them as well as I, and it ought not to have been impossible for me to be frank with him; but as yet I
could not trust any one with my secret hope of some
day living for literature, although I had already lived
for nothing else.   I preferred the disadvantage which
I must be at in his eyes, and in the eyes of most of
my fellow-citizens; I believe I had the applause of the
organ-builder, who thought the law no calling for me.

In that village there was a social equality which, if
not absolute, was as nearly so as can ever be in a com-
petitive civilization; and I could have suffered no
slight in the general esteem for giving up a profession
and going back to a trade; if I was despised at all it
was because I had thrown away the chance of material
advancement; I dare say some people thought I was a
fool to do that.   No one, indeed, could have imagined
the rapture it was to do it, or what a load rolled from
my shoulders when I dropped the law from them.
Perhaps Sinbad or Christian could have conceived of
my ecstatic relief; yet so far as the popular vision
reached I was not returning to literature, but to the
printing business, and I myself felt the difference.
My reading had given me criterions different from
those of the simple life of our village, and I did not

flatter myself that my calling would have been thought
one of great social dignity in the world where I hoped
some day to make my living. My convictions were
all democratic, but at heart I am afraid I was a snob,
and was unworthy of the honest work which I ought
to have felt it an honor to do ; this, whatever we
falsely pretend to the contrary, is the frame of every
one who aspires beyond the work of his hands. I do
not know how it had become mine, except through my
reading, and I think it was through the devotion I
then had for a certain author that I came to a knowledge not of good and evil so much as of common and
superfine.

XX.

THACKERAY.

It was of the organ-builder that I had Thackeray's
books first. He knew their literary quality, and their
rank in the literary world; but I believe he was surprised at the passion I instantly conceived for them.
He could not understand it; he deplored it almost as
a moral defect in me; though he honored it as a proof
of my critical taste. In a certain measure he was
right.

What flatters the worldly pride in a young man is
what fascinates him with Thackeray. With his air of
looking down on the highest, and confidentially in-
viting you to be of his company in the seat of the
scorner he is irresistible; his very confession that he
is a snob, too, is balm and solace to the reader who
secretly admires the splendors he affects to despise.
His sentimentality is also dear to the heart of youth,

and the boy who is dazzled by his satire is melted by his easy pathos. Then, if the boy has read a good many other books, he is taken with that abundance of literary turn and allusion in Thackeray; there is hardly a sentence but reminds him that he is in the society of a great literary swell, who has read everything, and can mock or burlesque life right and left from the literature always at his command. At the same time he feels his mastery, and is abjectly grateful to him in his own simple love of the good for his patronage of the unassuming virtues. It is so pleasing to one's vanity, and so safe, to be of the master's side when he assails those vices and foibles which are inherent in the system of things, and which one can contemn with vast applause so long as one does not attempt to undo the conditions they spring from.

I exulted to have Thackeray attack the aristocrats, and expose their wicked pride and meanness, and I never noticed that he did not propose to do away with aristocracy, which is and must always be just what it has been, and which cannot be changed while it exists at all. He appeared to me one of the noblest creatures that ever was when he derided the shams of society; and I was far from seeing that society, as we have it, was necessarily a sham; when he made a

mock of snobbishness I did not know but snobbishness was something that might be reached and cured
by ridicule. Now I know that so long as we have social inequality we shall have snobs; we shall have men
who bully and truckle, and women who snub and
crawl. I know that it is futile to spurn them, or lash
them for trying to get on in the world, and that the
world is what it must be from the selfish motives
which underlie our economic life. But I did not know
these things then, nor for long afterward, and so I
gave my heart to Thackeray, who seemed to promise
me in his contempt of the world a refuge from the
shame I felt for my own want of figure in it. He had
the effect of taking me into the great world, and making me a party to his splendid indifference to titles,
and even to royalties; and I could not see that sham
for sham he was unwittingly the greatest sham of all.

I think it was Pendennis I began with, and I lived
in the book to the very last line of it, and made its
alien circumstance mine to the smallest detail. I am
still not sure but it is the author's greatest book, and
I speak from a thorough acquaintance with every line
he has written, except the Virginians, which I have
never been able to read quite through; most of his
work I have read twice, and some of it twenty times.

After reading Pendennis I went to Vanity Fair, which I now think the poorest of Thackeray's novels —crude, heavy-handed, caricatured. About the same time I reveled in the romanticism of Henry Esmond, with its pseudo-eighteenth-century sentiment, and its appeals to an overwrought ideal of gentlemanhood and honor. It was long before I was duly revolted by Esmond's transfer of his passion from the daughter to the mother whom he is successively enamoured of. I believe this unpleasant and preposterous affair is thought one of the fine things in the story; I do not mind owning that I thought it so myself when I was seventeen; and if I could have found a Beatrix to be in love with, and a Lady Castlewood to be in love with me, I should have asked nothing finer of fortune. The glamour of Henry Esmond was all the deeper because I was reading the Spectator then, and was constantly in the company of Addison and Steele, and Swift, and Pope, and all the wits at Will's, who are presented evanescently in the romance. The intensely literary keeping, as well as quality, of the story I suppose is what formed its highest fascination for me; but that effect of great world which it imparts to the reader, making him citizen, and, if he will, leading citizen of it, was what helped turn my head.

This is the toxic property of all Thackeray's writing. He is himself forever dominated in imagination by the world, and even while he tells you it is not worth while he makes you feel that it is worth while. It is not the honest man, but the man of honor, who shines in his page; his meek folk are proudly meek, and there is a touch of superiority, a glint of mundane splendor, in his lowliest. He rails at the order of things, but he imagines nothing different, even when he shows that its baseness, and cruelty, and hypocrisy are well-nigh inevitable, and, for most of those who wish to get on in it, quite inevitable. He has a good word for the virtues, he patronizes the Christian graces, he pats humble merit on the head; he has even explosions of indignation against the insolence and pride of birth, and purse-pride. But, after all, he is of the world, worldly, and the highest hope he holds out is that you may be in the world and despise its ambitions while you compass its ends.

I should be far from blaming him for all this. He was of his time; but since his time men have thought beyond him, and seen life with a vision which makes his seem rather purblind. He must have been immensely in advance of most of the thinking and feeling of his day, for people then used to accuse his sentimental pessimism of cynical qualities which we could hardly find in it now. It was the age of intense individualism, when you were to do right because it was becoming to you, say, as a gentleman, and you were to have an eye single to the effect upon your character, if not your reputation; you were not to do a mean thing because it was wrong, but because it was mean. It was romanticism carried into the region of morals. But I had very little concern then as to that sort of error.

I was on a very high æsthetic horse, which I could not have conveniently stooped from if I had wished; it was quite enough for me that Thackeray's novels were prodigious works of art, and I acquired merit, at least with myself, for appreciating them so keenly, for liking them so much. It must be, I felt with far less consciousness than my formulation of the feeling expresses, that I was of some finer sort myself to be able to enjoy such a fine sort. No doubt I should have been a coxcomb of some kind, if not that kind, and I shall not be very strenuous in censuring Thackeray for his effect upon me in this way. No doubt the effect was already in me, and he did not so much produce it as find it.

In the meantime he was a vast delight to me, as

much in the variety of his minor works,—his Yellow-plush, and Letters of Mr. Brown, and Adventures of Major Gahagan, and the Paris Sketch Book, and the Irish Sketch Book, and the Great Hoggarty Diamond, and the Book of Snobs, and the English Humorists, and the Four Georges, and all the multitude of his essays, and verses, and caricatures,—as in the spacious designs of his huge novels, the Newcomes, and Pendennis, and Vanity Fair, and Henry Esmond, and Barry Lyndon.

There was something in the art of the last which seemed to me then, and still seems, the farthest reach of the author's great talent. It is couched, like so much of his work, in the autobiographic form, which next to the dramatic form is the most natural, and which lends itself with such flexibility to the purpose of the author. In Barry Lyndon there is imagined to the life a scoundrel of such rare quality that he never supposes for a moment but he is the finest sort of a gentleman; and so, in fact, he was, as most gentlemen went in his day. Of course, the picture is overcolored; it was the vice of Thackeray, or of Thackeray's time, to surcharge all imitations of life and character, so that a generation apparently much slower, if not duller than ours, should not possibly miss the artist's meaning. But I do not think it is so much surcharged as Esmond; Barry Lyndon is by no manner of means so conscious as that mirror of gentlemanhood, with its manifold self-reverberations; and for these reasons I am inclined to think he is the most perfect creation of Thackeray's mind.

I did not make the acquaintance of Thackeray's books all at once, or even in rapid succession, and he at no time possessed the whole empire of my catholic, not to say fickle, affections, during the years I was compassing a full knowledge and sense of his greatness, and burning incense at his shrine. But there was a moment when he so outshone and overtopped all other divinities in my worship that I was effectively his alone, as I have been the helpless and, as it were, hypnotized devotee of three or four others of the very great. From his art there flowed into me a literary quality which tinged my whole mental substance, and made it impossible for me to say, or wish to say, anything without giving it the literary color. That is, while he dominated my love and fancy, if I had been so fortunate as to have a simple concept of anything in life, I must have tried to give the expression of it some turn or tint that would remind the reader of books even before it reminded him of men.

It is hard to make out what I mean, but this is a try at it, and I do not know that I shall be able to do better unless I add that Thackeray, of all the writers that I have known, is the most thoroughly and profoundly imbued with literature, so that when he speaks it is not with words and blood, but with words and ink. You may read the greatest part of Dickens, as you may read the greatest part of Hawthorne or Tolstoy, and not once be reminded of literature as a business or a cult, but you can hardly read a paragraph, hardly a sentence, of Thackeray's without being reminded of it either by suggestion or downright allusion.

I do not blame him for this; he was himself, and he could not have been any other manner of man without loss; but I say that the greatest talent is not that which breathes of the library, but that which breathes of the street, the field, the open sky, the simple earth. I began to imitate this master of mine almost as soon as I began to read him; this must be, and I had a greater pride and joy in my success than I should probably have known in anything really creative; I should have suspected that, I should have distrusted that, because I had nothing to test it by, no model; but here before me was the very finest and noblest model, and I had but to form my lines upon it, and I had produced a work of art altogether more estimable in my eyes than anything else could have been. I saw the little world about me through the lenses of my master's spectacles, and I reported its facts, in his tone and his attitude, with his self-flattered scorn, his showy sighs, his facile satire. I need not say I was perfectly satisfied with the result, or that to be able to imitate Thackeray was a much greater thing for me than to have been able to imitate nature. In fact, I could have valued any picture of the life and character I knew only as it put me in mind of life and character as these had shown themselves to me in his books.

XXI.

LAZARILLO DE TORMES.

AT the same time, I was not only reading many books besides Thackeray's, but I was studying to get a smattering of several languages as well as I could, with or without help. I could now manage Spanish fairly well, and I was sending on to New York for authors in that tongue. I do not remember how I got the money to buy them; to be sure it was no great sum; but it must have been given me out of the sums we were all working so hard to make up for the debt, and the interest on the debt (that is always the wicked pinch for the debtor!), we had incurred in the purchase of the newspaper which we lived by, and the house which we lived in. I spent no money on any other sort of pleasure, and so, I suppose, it was afforded me the more readily; but I cannot really recall the history of those acquisitions on its financial side.

In any case, if the sums I laid out in literature could not have been comparatively great, the excitement attending the outlay was prodigious.

I know that I used to write on to Messrs. Roe Lockwood & Son, New York, for my Spanish books, and I dare say that my letters were sufficiently pedantic, and filled with a simulated acquaintance with all Spanish literature. Heaven knows what they must have thought, if they thought anything, of their queer customer in that obscure little Ohio village; but he could not have been queerer to them than to his fellow-villagers, I am sure. I haunted the post-office about the time the books were due, and when I found one of them in our deep box among a heap of exchange newspapers and business letters, my emotion was so great that it almost took my breath. I hurried home with the precious volume, and shut myself into my little den, where I gave myself up to a sort of transport in it. These books were always from the collection of Spanish authors published by Baudry in Paris, and they were in saffron-colored paper covers, printed full of a perfectly intoxicating catalogue of other Spanish books which I meant to read, every one, some time. The paper and the ink had a certain odor which was sweeter to me than the perfumes of Araby.

The look of the type took me more than the glance of
a girl, and I had a fever of longing to know the heart
of the book, which was like a lover's passion. Sometimes I did not reach its heart, but commonly I did.
Moratin's Origins of the Spanish Theatre, and a large
volume of Spanish dramatic authors, were the first
Spanish books I sent for, but I could not say why I
sent for them, unless it was because I saw that there
were some plays of Cervantes among the rest. I read
these and I read several comedies of Lope de Vega,
and numbers of archaic dramas in Moratin's history,
and I really got a fairish perspective of the Spanish
drama, which has now almost wholly faded from my
mind. It is more intelligible to me why I should have
read Condé's Dominion of the Arabs in Spain; for
that was in the line of my reading in Irving, which
would account for my pleasure in the History of the
Civil Wars of Granada; it was some time before I
realized that the chronicles in this were a bundle of romances and not veritable records; and my whole study
in these things was wholly undirected and unenlight-
ened. But I meant to be thorough in it, and I could
not rest satisfied with the Spanish-English grammars
I had; I was not willing to stop short of the official
grammar of the Spanish Academy. I sent to New

York for it, and my bookseller there reported that
they would have to send to Spain for it. I lived till
it came to hand through them from Madrid; and I do
not understand why I did not perish then from the
pride and joy I had in it.

But, after all, I am not a Spanish scholar, and can
neither speak nor write the language. I never got more
than a good reading use of it, perhaps because I never
really tried for more. But I am very glad of that,
because it has been a great pleasure to me, and even
some profit, and it has lighted up many meanings in
literature, which must always have remained dark to
me. Not to speak now of the modern Spanish writers
whom it has enabled me to know in their own houses
as it were, I had even in that remote day a rapturous
delight in a certain Spanish book, which was well
worth all the pains I had undergone to get at it. This
was the famous picaresque novel, Lazarillo de Tormes,
by Hurtado de Mendoza, whose name then so famil-
iarized itself to my fondness that now as I write it I
feel as if it were that of an old personal friend whom
I had known in the flesh. I believe it would not have
been always comfortable to know Mendoza outside of
his books; he was rather a terrible person; he was
one of the Spanish invaders of Italy, and is known in

Italian history as the Tyrant of Siena. But at my distance of time and place I could safely revel in his friendship, and as an author I certainly found him a most charming companion. The adventures of his rogue of a hero, who began life as the servant and ac-complice of a blind beggar, and then adventured on through a most diverting career of knavery, brought back the atmosphere of Don Quixote, and all the land-scape of that dear wonder-world of Spain, where I had lived so much, and I followed him with all the old delight.

I do not know that I should counsel others to do so, or that the general reader would find his account in it, but I am sure that the intending author of American fiction would do well to study the Spanish picaresque novels; for in their simplicity of design he will find one of the best forms for an American story. The intrigue of close texture will never suit our con-ditions, which are so loose and open and variable; each man's life among us is a romance of the Spanish model, if it is the life of a man who has risen, as we nearly all have, with many ups and downs. The story of Lazarillo is gross in its facts, and is mostly "un-meet for ladies," like most of the fiction in all lan-guages before our times; but there is an honest sim-

plicity in the narration, a pervading humor, and a rich
feeling for character that gives it value.

I think that a good deal of its foulness was lost
upon me, but I certainly understood that it would not
do to present it to an American public just as it was,
in the translation which I presently planned to make.
I went about telling the story to people, and trying to
make them find it as amusing as I did, but whether I
ever succeeded I cannot say, though the notion of a
version with modifications constantly grew with me,
till one day I went to the city of Cleveland with my
father.   There was a branch house of an Eastern firm
of publishers in that place, and I must have had the
hope that I might have the courage to propose a translation of Lazarillo to them.   My father urged me to
try my fortune, but my heart failed me.   I was half
blind with one of the headaches that tormented me in
those days, and I turned my sick eyes from the sign,
" J. P. Jewett & Co., Publishers," which held me fascinated, and went home without at least having my
much-dreamed-of version of Lazarillo refused.

XXII.

CURTIS, LONGFELLOW, SCHLEGEL.

I AM quite at a loss to know why my reading had this direction or that in those days. It had necessarily passed beyond my father's suggestion, and I think it must have been largely by accident or experiment that I read one book rather than another. He made some sort of newspaper arrangement with a book-store in Cleveland, which was the means of enriching our home library with a goodly number of books, shopworn, but none the worse for that, and new in the only way that books need be new to the lover of them. Among these I found a treasure in Curtis's two books, the Nile Notes of a Howadji, and the Howadji in Syria. I already knew him by his Potiphar Papers, and the ever-delightful reveries which have since gone under the name of Prue and I; but those books of Eastern travel opened a new world of

thinking and feeling.   They had at once a great influence upon me.   The smooth richness of their diction;
the amiable sweetness of their mood, their gracious
caprice, the delicacy of their satire (which was so kind
that it should have some other name), their abundance
of light and color, and the deep heart of humanity
underlying their airiest fantasticality, all united in an
effect which was different from any I had yet known.

As usual, I steeped myself in them, and the first
runnings of my fancy when I began to pour it out
afterward were of their flavor.   I tried to write like
this new master; but whether I had tried or not, I
should probably have done so from the love I bore
him.   As I have hinted, he was already a favorite of
mine, and of all the young people in the village who
were reading current literature, so that on this ground
at least I had abundant sympathy.   The present generation can have little notion of the deep impression
made upon the intelligence and conscience of the whole
nation by the Potiphar Papers, or how its fancy was
rapt with the Prue and I sketches.   These are among
the most veritable literary successes we have had, and
probably we who were so glad when the author of
these beautiful things turned aside from the flowery
paths where he led us, to battle for freedom in the

field of politics, would have felt the sacrifice too great if we could have dreamed it would be life-long. But, as it was, we could only honor him the more, and give him a place in our hearts which he shares with Longfellow alone.

This divine poet I have never ceased to read. His Hiawatha was a new book during one of those terrible Lake Shore winters, but all the other poems were old friends with me by that time. With a sister who is no longer living I had a peculiar devotion for his pretty and touching and lightly humorous tale of Kavanagh, which was of a village life enough like our own, in some things, to make us know the truth of its delicate realism. We used to read it and talk it fondly over together, and I believe some stories of like make and manner grew out of our pleasure in it. They were never finished, but it was enough to begin them, and there were few writers, if any, among those I delighted in who escaped the tribute of an imitation. One has to begin that way, or at least one had in my day; perhaps it is now possible for a young writer to begin by being himself; but for my part, that was not half so important as to be like some one else. Literature, not life, was my aim, and to reproduce it was my joy and my pride.

I was widening my knowledge of it helplessly and involuntarily, and I was always chancing upon some book that served this end among the great number of books that I read merely for my pleasure without any real result of the sort. Schlegel's Lectures on Dramatic Literature came into my hands not long after I had finished my studies in the history of the Spanish theatre, and it made the whole subject at once luminous. I cannot give a due notion of the comfort this book afforded me by the light it cast upon paths where I had dimly made my way before, but which I now followed in the full day.

Of course, I pinned my faith to everything that Schlegel said. I obediently despised the classic unities and the French and Italian theatre which had perpetuated them, and I revered the romantic drama which had its glorious course among the Spanish and English poets, and which was crowned with the fame of the Cervantes and the Shakespeare whom I seemed to own, they owned me so completely. It vexes me now to find that I cannot remember how the book came into my hands, or who could have suggested it to me. It is possible that it may have been that artist who came and stayed a month with us while she painted my mother's portrait. She was fresh from her studies

in New York, where she had met authors and artists
at the house of the Carey sisters, and had even once
seen my adored Curtis somewhere, though she had
not spoken with him.   Her talk about these things
simply emparadised me; it lifted me into a heaven of
hope that I, too, might some day meet such elect spirits and converse with them face to face.   My mood
was sufficiently foolish, but it was not such a frame of
mind as I can be ashamed of; and I could wish a boy
no happier fortune than to possess it for a time, at
least.

XXIII.

TENNYSON.

I CANNOT quite see now how I found time for even trying to do the things I had in hand more or less. It is perfectly clear to me that I did none of them well, though I meant at the time to do none of them other than excellently. I was attempting the study of no less than four languages, and I presently added a fifth to these. I was reading right and left in every direction, but chiefly in that of poetry, criticism and fiction. From time to time I boldly attacked a history, and carried it by a *coup de main*, or sat down before it for a prolonged siege. There was occasionally an author who worsted me, whom I tried to read and quietly gave up after a vain struggle, but I must say that these authors were few. I had got a very fair notion of the range of all literature, and the relations of the different literatures to one another, and I knew pretty well what manner of book it was that I took up before I committed myself to the task of reading it. Always I read for pleasure, for the delight of knowing something more; and this pleasure is a very different thing from amusement, though I read a great deal for mere amusement, as I do still, and to take my mind away from unhappy or harassing thoughts. There are very few things that I think it a waste of time to have read; I should probably have wasted the time if I had not read them, and at the period I speak of I do not think I wasted much time.

My day began about seven o'clock, in the printing-office, where it took me till noon to do my task of so many thousand ems, say four or five. Then we had dinner, after the simple fashion of people who work with their hands for their dinners. In the afternoon I went back and corrected the proof of the type I had set and distributed my case for the next day. At two or three o'clock I was free, and then I went home and began my studies; or tried to write something; or read a book. We had supper at six, and after that I rejoiced in literature, till I went to bed at ten or eleven. I cannot think of any time when I did not go gladly to my books or manuscripts, when it was not a noble joy as well as a high privilege.

But it all ended as such a strain must, in the sort of break which was not yet known as nervous prostration. When I could not sleep after my studies, and the sick headaches came oftener, and then days and weeks of hypochondriacal misery, it was apparent I was not well; but that was not the day of anxiety for such things, and if it was thought best that I should leave work and study for a while, it was not with the notion that the case was at all serious, or needed an uninterrupted cure. I passed days in the woods and fields, gunning or picking berries; I spent myself in heavy work; I made little journeys; and all this was very wholesome and very well; but I did not give up my reading or my attempts to write. No doubt I was secretly proud to have been invalided in so great a cause, and to be sicklied over with the pale cast of thought, rather than by some ignoble ague or the devastating consumption of that region. If I lay awake, noting the wild pulsations of my heart, and listening to the death-watch in the wall, I was certainly very much scared, but I was not without the consolation that I was at least a sufferer for literature. At the same time that I was so horribly afraid of dying, I could have composed an epitaph which would have moved others to tears for my untimely fate. But there was really no impairment of my constitution, and after a while I began to be better, and little by little the health which has never since failed me under any reasonable stress of work established itself.

I was in the midst of this unequal struggle when I first became acquainted with the poet who at once possessed himself of what was best worth having in me. Probably I knew of Tennyson by extracts, and from the English reviews, but I believe it was from reading one of Curtis's Easy Chair papers that I was prompted to get the new poem of Maud, which I understood from the Easy Chair was then moving polite youth in the East. It did not seem to me that I could very well live without that poem, and when I went to Cleveland with the hope that I might have courage to propose a translation of Lazarillo to a publisher it was with the fixed purpose of getting Maud if it was to be found in any bookstore there.

I do not know why I was so long in reaching Tennyson, and I can only account for it by the fact that I was always reading rather the earlier than the later English poetry. To be sure I had passed through what I may call a paroxysm of Alexander Smith, a poet deeply unknown to the present generation, but then acclaimed immortal by all the critics, and put with Shakespeare, who must be a good deal astonished from time to time in his Elysian quiet by the companionship thrust upon him.   I read this now dead-and-gone immortal with an ecstasy unspeakable; I raved of him by day, and dreamed of him by night; I got great lengths of his Life-Drama by heart, and I can still repeat several gorgeous passages from it; I would almost have been willing to take the life of the sole critic who had the sense to laugh at him, and who made his wicked fun in Graham's Magazine, an extinct periodical of the old extinct Philadelphian species. I cannot tell how I came out of this craze, but neither could any of the critics who led me into it, I dare say. The reading world is very susceptible of such lunacies, and all that can be said is that at a given time it was time for criticism to go mad over a poet who was neither better nor worse than many another third-rate poet apotheosized before and since.   What was good in Smith was the reflected fire of the poets who had a vital heat in them ; and it was by mere chance that I bathed myself in his second-hand effulgence.   I already knew pretty well the origin of the Tennysonian line in English poetry ; Wordsworth, and Keats, and Shelley; and I did not come to Tennyson's worship a sudden convert, but my devotion to him was none the less complete and exclusive. Like every other great poet he somehow expressed the feelings of his day, and I suppose that at the time he wrote Maud he said more fully what the whole English-speaking race were then dimly longing to utter than any English poet who has lived.

One need not question the greatness of Browning in owning the fact that the two poets of his day who pre-eminently voiced their generation were Tennyson and Longfellow; though Browning, like Emerson, is probably now more modern than either. However, I had then nothing to do with Tennyson's comparative claim on my adoration; there was for the time no parallel for him in the whole range of literary divinities that I had bowed the knee to. For that while, the temple was not only emptied of all the other idols, but I had a richly flattering illusion of being his only worshiper. When I came to the sense of this error, it was with the belief that at least no one else had ever appreciated him so fully, stood so close to him in that holy of holies where he wrought his miracles.

I say tawdrily and ineffectively and falsely what was a very precious and sacred experience with me. This great poet opened to me a whole world of thinking and feeling, where I had my being with him in that mystic intimacy which cannot be put into words. I at once identified myself not only with the hero of the poem, but in some sort with the poet himself, when I read Maud; but that was only the first step toward the lasting state in which his poetry has upon the whole been more to me than that of any other poet. I have never read any other so closely and continuously, or read myself so much into and out of his verse. There have been times and moods when I have had my questions, and made my cavils, and when it seemed to me that the poet was less than I had thought him; and certainly I do not revere equally and unreservedly all that he has written; that would be impossible. But when I think over all the other poets I have read, he is supreme above them in his response to some need in me that he has satisfied so perfectly.

Of course, Maud seemed to me the finest poem I had read, up to that time, but I am not sure that this conclusion was wholly my own; I think it was partially formed for me by the admiration of the poem which I felt to be everywhere in the critical atmosphere, and which had already penetrated to me. I did not like all parts of it equally well, and some parts of it seemed thin and poor (though I would not suffer

myself to say so then), and they still seem so. But
there were whole passages and spaces of it whose divine and perfect beauty lifted me above life. I did
not fully understand the poem then; I do not fully
understand it now, but that did not and does not matter; for there is something in poetry that reaches the
soul by other avenues than the intelligence. Both in
this poem and others of Tennyson, and in every poet
that I have loved, there are melodies and harmonies
enfolding a significance that appeared long after I had
first read them, and had even learned them by heart;
that lay sweetly in my outer ear and were enough in
their mere beauty of phrasing, till the time came for
them to reveal their whole meaning. In fact they
could do this only to later and greater knowledge of
myself and others, as every one must recognize who
recurs in after-life to a book that he read when young;
then he finds it twice as full of meaning as it was at
first.

I could not rest satisfied with Maud; I sent the
same summer to Cleveland for the little volume which
then held all the poet's work, and abandoned myself
so wholly to it, that for a year I read no other verse
that I can remember. The volume was the first of
that pretty blue-and-gold series which Ticknor &

Fields began to publish in 1856, and which their im-
print, so rarely affixed to an unworthy book, at once
carried far and wide.   Their modest old brown cloth
binding had long been a quiet warrant of quality in
the literature it covered, and now this splendid blossom of the book-making art, as it seemed, was fitly
employed to convey the sweetness and richness of the
loveliest poetry that I thought the world had yet
known.   After an old fashion of mine, I read it continuously, with frequent recurrences from each new
poem to some that had already pleased me, and with
a most capricious range among the pieces.   In Memoriam was in that book, and the Princess; I read
the Princess through and through, and over and over,
but I did not then read In Memoriam through, and I
have never read it in course; I am not sure that I have
even yet read every part of it.   I did not come to the
Princess, either, until I had saturated my fancy and
my memory with some of the shorter poems, with the
Dream of Fair Women, with the Lotus Eaters, with
the Miller's Daughter, with the Morte d'Arthur, with
Edwin Morris or The Lake, with Love and Duty, and
a score of other minor and briefer poems.   I read the
book night and day, indoors and out, to myself and to
whomever I could make listen.   I have no words to

tell the rapture it was to me; but I hope that in some more articulate being, if it should ever be my unmerited fortune to meet that *sommo poeta* face to face, it shall somehow be uttered from me to him, and he will understand how completely he became the life of the boy I was then. I think it might please, or at least amuse, that lofty ghost, and that he would not resent it, as he would probably have done on earth. . I can well understand why the homage of his worshipers should have afflicted him here, and I could never have been one to burn incense in his presence; but perhaps it might be done hereafter without offense. I eagerly caught up and treasured every personal word I could find about him, and I dwelt in that sort of charmed intimacy with him through his verse, in which I could not presume nor he repel, and which I had enjoyed in turn with Cervantes and Shakespeare, without a snub from them.

I have never ceased to adore Tennyson, though the rapture of the new convert could not last. That must pass like the flush of any other passion. I think I have now a better sense of his comparative greatness, but a better sense of his positive greatness I could not have than I had at the beginning; and I believe this is the essential knowledge of a poet. It is very well to say one is greater than Keats, or not so great as Wordsworth; that one is or is not of the highest order of poets like Shakespeare and Dante and Goethe; but that does not mean anything of value, and I never find my account in it. I know it is not possible for any less than the greatest writer to abide lastingly in one's life. Some dazzling comer may enter and possess it for a day, but he soon wears his welcome out, and presently finds the door, to be answered with a not-at-home if he knocks again. But it was only this morning that I read one of the new last poems of Tennyson with a return of the emotion which he first woke in me well-nigh forty years ago. There has been no year of those many when I have not read him and loved him with something of the early fire if not all the early conflagration; and each successive poem of his has been for me a fresh joy.

He went with me into the world from my village when I left it to make my first venture away from home. My father had got one of those legislative clerkships which used to fall sometimes to deserving country editors when their party was in power, and we together imagined and carried out a scheme for corresponding with some city newspapers. We were to furnish a daily letter giving an account of the legislative proceedings, which I was mainly to write up from material he helped me to get together. The letters at once found favor with the editors who agreed to take them, and my father then withdrew from the work altogether, after telling them who was doing it. We were afraid they might not care for the reports of a boy of nineteen, but they did not seem to take my age into account, and I did not boast of my youth among the law-makers. I had a mustache that came early and black, and I looked three or four years older than I was; but I experienced a terrible moment once when a fatherly Senator asked me my age. I got away somehow without saying, but it was a great relief to me when my twentieth birthday came that winter, and I could honestly proclaim that I was in my twenty-first year.

I had now the free range of the State Library, and I drew many sorts of books from it. Largely, however, they were fiction, and I read all the novels of Bulwer, for whom I had already a great liking from The Caxtons and My Novel. I was dazzled by them, and I thought him a great writer, if not so great a one as he thought himself. Little or nothing of those romances, with their swelling prefaces about the poet and his function, their glittering criminals, and showy

rakes and rogues of all kinds, and their patrician perfume and social splendor, remained with me; they may
have been better or worse; I will not attempt to say.
If I may call my fascination with them a passion at all,
I must say that it was but a fitful fever. I also read
many volumes of Zschokke's admirable tales, which I
found in a translation in the Library, and I think I
began at the same time to find out De Quincey. These
authors I recall out of the many that passed through
my mind almost as tracelessly as they passed through
my hands. I got at some versions of Icelandic poems,
in the metre of Hiawatha; I had for a while a notion
of studying Icelandic, and I did take out an Icelandic
grammar and lexicon, and decided that I would learn
the language later. By this time I must have begun
German, which I afterward carried so far, with one
author at least, as to find in him a delight only second
to that I had in Tennyson; but as yet Tennyson was
all in all to me in poetry. I suspect that I carried his
poems about with me a great part of the time; I am
certain that I always had that blue-and-gold Tennyson
in my pocket; and I was ready to draw it upon anybody at the slightest provocation. This is the worst of
the ardent lover of literature: he wishes to make every
one else share his rapture, will he, nill he. Many good

fellows suffered from my admiration of this author or that, and many more pretty, patient maids. I wanted to read my favorite passages, my favorite poems to them; I am afraid I often did read, when they would rather have been talking; in the case of the poems I did worse, I repeated them. This seems rather incredible now, but it is true enough, and absurd as it is, it at least attests my sincerity. It was long before I cured myself of so pestilent a habit; and I am not yet so perfectly well of it that I could be safely trusted with a fascinating book and a submissive listener.

I dare say I could not have been made to understand at this time that Tennyson was not so nearly the first interest of life with other people as he was with me; I must often have suspected it, but I was helpless against the wish to make them feel him as important to their prosperity and well-being as he was to mine. My head was full of him; his words were always behind my lips; and when I was not repeating his phrase to myself or to some one else, I was trying to frame something of my own as like him as I could. It was a time of melancholy from ill-health, and of anxiety for the future in which I must make my own place in the world. Work, and hard work, I had always been used to and never afraid of; but work is by no means the whole story. You may get on without much of it, or you may do a great deal, and not get on. I was willing to do as much of it as I could get to do, but I distrusted my health, somewhat, and I had many forebodings, which my adored poet helped me to transfigure to the substance of literature, or enabled me for the time to forget. I was already imitating him in the verse I wrote; he now seemed the only worthy model for one who meant to be as great a poet as I did. None of the authors whom I read at all displaced him in my devotion, and I could not have believed that any other poet would ever be so much to me. In fact, as I have expressed, none ever has been.

XXIV.

HEINE.

THAT winter passed very quickly and happily for me, and at the end of the legislative session I had acquitted myself so much to the satisfaction of one of the newspapers which I wrote for that I was offered a place on it. I was asked to be city editor, as it was called in that day, and I was to have charge of the local reporting. It was a great temptation, and for a while I thought it the greatest piece of good fortune. I went down to Cincinnati to acquaint myself with the details of the work, and to fit myself for it by beginning as reporter myself. One night's round of the police stations with the other reporters satisfied me that I was not meant for that work, and I attempted it no farther. I have often been sorry since, for it would have made known to me many phases of life that I have always remained ignorant of, but I did not know then that life was supremely interesting and important. I fancied that literature, that poetry was so; and it was humiliation and anguish indescribable to think of myself torn from my high ideals by labors like those of the reporter. I would not consent even to do the office work of the department, so much had I a soul above buttons, and the proprietor and editor who was more especially my friend tried to make some other place for me. All the departments were full but the one I would have nothing to do with, and after a few weeks of sufferance and suffering I turned my back on a thousand dollars a year, and for the second time returned to the printing-office.

I was glad to get home, for I had been all the time tormented by my old malady of homesickness. But otherwise the situation was not cheerful for me, and I now began trying to write something for publication that I could sell. I sent off poems and they came back; I offered little translations from the Spanish that nobody wanted. At the same time I took up the study of German, which I must have already played with, at such odd times as I could find. My father knew something of it, and that friend of mine among the printers was already reading it and trying to speak it. I had their help with the first steps so far as the recitations from Ollendorff were concerned, but I was impatient to read German, or rather to read one German poet who had seized my fancy from the first line of his I had seen.

This poet was Heinrich Heine, who dominated me longer than any one author that I have known. Where or when I first acquainted myself with his most fascinating genius, I cannot be sure, but I think it was in some article of the Westminster Review, where several poems of his were given in English and German; and their singular beauty and grace at once possessed my soul. I was in a fever to know more of him, and it was my great good luck to fall in with a German in the village who had his books. He was a bookbinder, one of those educated artisans whom the revolutions of 1848 sent to us in great numbers. He was a Hanoverian, and his accent was then, I believe, the standard, though the Berlinese is now the accepted pronunciation. But I cared very little for accent; my wish was to get at Heine with as little delay as possible ; and I began to cultivate the friendship of that bookbinder in every way. I dare say he was glad of mine, for he was otherwise quite alone in the village, or had no companionship outside of his own family. I clothed him in all the romantic interest I began to feel for his

race and language, which now took the place of the
Spaniards and Spanish in my affections.   He was a
very quick and gay intelligence, with more sympathy
for my love of our author's humor than for my love
of his sentiment, and I can remember very well the
twinkle of his little sharp black eyes, with their Tar-
tar slant, and the twitching of his keenly-pointed, sensitive nose, when we came to some passage of biting
satire, or some phrase in which the bitter Jew had
unpacked all the insult of his soul.

We began to read Heine together when my vocabulary had to be dug almost word by word out of the
dictionary, for the bookbinder's English was rather
scanty at the best, and was not literary.   As for the
grammar, I was getting that up as fast as I could
from Ollendorff, and from other sources, but I was
enjoying Heine before I well knew a declension or a
conjugation.   As soon as my task was done at the
office, I went home to the books, and worked away at
them until supper.   Then my bookbinder and I met
in my father's editorial room, and with a couple of
candles on the table between us, and our Heine and
the dictionary before us, we read till we were both
tired out.

The candles were tallow, and they lopped at different angles in the flat candle-sticks, heavily loaded with lead, which compositors once used. It seems to have been summer when our readings began, and they are associated in my memory with the smell of the neighboring gardens, which came in at the open doors and windows, and with the fluttering of moths, and bumbling of the dorbugs, that stole in along with the odors. I can see the perspiration on the shining forehead of the bookbinder as he looks up from some brilliant passage, to exchange a smile of triumph with me at having made out the meaning with the meagre facilities we had for the purpose; he had beautiful red pouting lips, and a stiff little branching mustache above them, that went to the making of his smile. Sometimes, in the truce we made with the text, he told a little story of his life at home, or some anecdote relevant to our reading, or quoted a passage from some other author. It seemed to me the make of a high intellectual banquet, and I should be glad if I could enjoy anything as much now.

We walked home as far as his house, or rather his apartment over one of the village stores; and as he mounted to it by an outside staircase, we exchanged a joyous "Gute Nacht," and I kept on homeward through the dark and silent village street, which was

really not that street, but some other, where Heine
had been, some street out of the Reisebilder, of his
knowledge or of his dream. When I reached home
it was useless to go to bed. I shut myself into my
little study, and went over what we had read, till my
brain was so full of it that when I crept up to my
room at last, it was to lie down to slumbers which
were often a mere phantasmagory of those witching
Pictures of Travel.

I was awake at my father's call in the morning, and
before my mother had breakfast ready I had recited
my lesson in Ollendorff to him. To tell the truth I
hated those grammatical studies, and nothing but the
love of literature, and the hope of getting at it, could
ever have made me go through them. Naturally, I
never got any scholarly use of the languages I was
worrying at, and though I could once write a passable
literary German, it has all gone from me now, except
for the purposes of reading. It cost me so much
trouble, however, to dig the sense out of the grammar
and lexicon, as I went on with the authors I was impatient to read, that I remember the words very well
in all their forms and inflections, and I have still what
I think I may call a fair German vocabulary.

The German of Heine, when once you are in the

joke of his capricious genius, is very simple, and in his poetry it is simple from the first, so that he was, perhaps, the best author I could have fallen in with if I wanted to go fast rather than far. I found this out later, when I attempted other German authors without the glitter of his wit or the lambent glow of his fancy to light me on my hard way. I should find it hard to say just why his peculiar genius had such an absolute fascination for me from the very first, and perhaps I had better content myself with saying simply that my literary liberation began with almost the earliest word from him; for if he chained me to himself he freed me from all other bondage. I had been at infinite pains from time to time, now upon one model and now upon another, to literarify myself, if I may make a word which does not quite say the thing for me. What I mean is that I had supposed, with the sense at times that I was all wrong, that the expression of literature must be different from the expression of life; that it must be an attitude, a pose, with something of state or at least of formality in it; that it must be this style, and not that; that it must be like that sort of acting which you know is acting when you see it and never mistake for reality. There are a great many children, apparently grown-up, and

largely accepted as critical authorities, who are still
of this youthful opinion of mine. But Heine at once
showed me that this ideal of literature was false ; that
the life of literature was from the springs of the best
common speech, and that the nearer it could be made
to conform, in voice, look and gait, to graceful, easy,
picturesque and humorous or impassioned talk, the
better it was.

He did not impart these truths without imparting
certain tricks with them, which I was careful to imitate as soon as I began to write in his manner, that is
to say instantly. His tricks he had mostly at second-
hand, and mainly from Sterne, whom I did not know
well enough then to know their origin. But in all es-
sentials he was himself, and my final lesson from him,
or the final effect of all my lessons from him, was to
find myself, and to be for good or evil whatsoever I
really was.

I kept on writing as much like Heine as I could for
several years, though, and for a much longer time than
I should have done if I had ever become equally impassioned of any other author. Some traces of his
method lingered so long in my work that nearly ten
years afterward Mr. Lowell wrote me about something
of mine that he had been reading: " You must sweat

the Heine out of your bones as men do mercury," and
his kindness for me would not be content with less
than the entire expulsion of the poison that had in its
good time saved my life. I dare say it was all well
enough not to have it in my bones after it had done
its office, but it did do its office.

It was in some prose sketch of mine that his keen
analysis had found the Heine, but the foreign property had been so prevalent in my earlier work in verse
that he kept the first contribution he accepted from
me for the Atlantic Monthly a long time, or long
enough to make sure that it was not a translation of
Heine. Then he printed it, and I am bound to say
that the poem now justifies his doubt to me, insomuch
that I do not see why Heine should not have had the
name of writing it if he had wanted. His potent spirit became immediately so wholly my "control," as the
mediums say, that my poems might as well have been
communications from him so far as any authority of
my own was concerned; and they were quite like
other inspirations from the other world in being so
inferior to the work of the spirit before it had the
misfortune to be disembodied and obliged to use a
medium. But I do not think that either Heine or I
had much lasting harm from it, and I am sure that

the good, in my case at least, was one that can only
end with me. He undid my hands, which I had taken
so much pains to tie behind my back, and he forever
persuaded me that though it may be ingenious and
surprising to dance in chains, it is neither pretty nor
useful.

XXV

ANOTHER author who was a prime favorite with me about this time was De Quincey, whose books I took out of the State Library, one after another, until I had read them all. We who were young people of that day thought his style something wonderful, and so indeed it was, especially in those passages, abundant everywhere in his work, relating to his own life with an intimacy which was always more rather than less. His rhetoric there, and in certain of his historical studies, had a sort of luminous richness, without losing its colloquial ease. I keenly enjoyed this subtle spirit, and the play of that brilliant intelligence which lighted up so many ways of literature with its lambent glow or its tricksy glimmer, and I had a deep sympathy with certain morbid moods and experiences so like my own, as I was pleased to fancy. I have not looked

at his Twelve Cæsars for twice as many years, but I
should be greatly surprised to find it other than one of
the greatest historical monographs ever written.   His
literary criticisms seemed to me not only exquisitely
humorous, but perfectly sane and just; and it delighted me to have him personally present, with the
warmth of his own temperament in regions of cold
abstraction; I am not sure that I should like that so
much now.   De Quincey was hardly less autobiograph-
ical when he wrote of Kant, or Flight of the Crim-Tar-
tars, than when he wrote of his own boyhood or the
miseries of the opium habit.   He had the hospitable
gift of making you at home with him, and appealing
to your sense of comradery with something of the
flattering confidentiality of Thackeray, but with a
wholly different effect.

In fact, although De Quincey was from time to time
perfunctorily Tory, and always a good and faithful
subject, he was so eliminated from his time and place
by his single love for books, that one could be in his
company through the whole vast range of his writings,
and come away without a touch of snobbishness; and
that is saying a great deal for an English writer.   He
was a great little creature, and through his intense
personality he achieved a sort of impersonality, so

that you loved the man, who was forever talking of himself, for his modesty and reticence. He left you feeling intimate with him but by no means familiar; with all his frailties, and with all those freedoms he permitted himself with the lives of his contemporaries, he is to me a figure of delicate dignity, and winning kindness. I think it a misfortune for the present generation that his books have fallen into a kind of neglect, and I believe that they will emerge from it again to the advantage of literature.

In spite of Heine and Tennyson, De Quincey had a large place in my affections, though this was perhaps because he was not a poet; for more than those two great poets there was then not much room. I read him the first winter I was at Columbus, and when I went down from the village the next winter, to take up my legislative correspondence again, I read him more than ever. But that was destined to be for me a very disheartening time. I had just passed through a rheumatic fever, which left my health more broken than before, and one morning shortly after I was settled in the capital, I woke to find the room going round me like a wheel. It was the beginning of a vertigo which lasted for six months, and which I began to fight with various devices and must yield to at last. I tried med-

icine and exercise, but it was useless, and my father
came to take my letters off my hands while I gave myself some ineffectual respites. I made a little journey
to my old home in southern Ohio, but there and everywhere, the sure and firm-set earth waved and billowed
under my feet, and I came back to Columbus and tried
to forget in my work the fact that I was no better. I
did not give up trying to read, as usual, and part of
my endeavor that winter was with Schiller, and Uhland, and even Goethe, whose Wahlverwandschaften
hardly yielded up its mystery to me. To tell the
truth, I do not think that I found my account in that
novel. It must needs be a disappointment after Wilhelm Meister, which I had read in English; but I dare
say my disappointment was largely my own fault; I
had certainly no right to expect such constant proofs
and instances of wisdom in Goethe as the unwisdom
of his critics had led me to hope for. I remember little or nothing of the story, which I tried to find very
memorable, as I held my sick way through it. Longfellow's Miles Standish came out that winter, and I
suspect that I got vastly more real pleasure from that
one poem of his than I found in all my German authors put together, the adored Heine always excepted;
though certainly I felt the romantic beauty of Uhland,

and was aware of something of Schiller's generous grandeur.

Of the American writers Longfellow has been most a passion with me, as the English, and German, and Spanish, and Russian writers have been. I am sure that this was largely by mere chance. It was because I happened, in such a frame and at such a time, to come upon his books that I loved them above those of other men as great. I am perfectly sensible that Lowell and Emerson outvalue many of the poets and prophets I have given my heart to; I have read them with delight and with a deep sense of their greatness, and yet they have not been my life like those other, those lesser, men. But none of the passions are reasoned, and I do not try to account for my literary preferences or to justify them.

I dragged along through several months of that winter, and did my best to carry out that notable scheme of not minding my vertigo. I tried doing half-work, and helping my father with the correspondence, but when it appeared that nothing would avail, he remained in charge of it, till the close of the session, and I went home to try what a complete and prolonged rest would do for me. I was not fit for work in the printing-office, but that was a simpler matter than the literary work that was always tempting me. I could get away from it only by taking my gun and tramping day after day through the deep, primeval woods. The fatigue was wholesome, and I was so bad a shot that no other creature suffered loss from my gain except one hapless wild pigeon. The thawing snow left the fallen beechnuts of the autumn before uncovered among the dead leaves, and the forest was full of the beautiful birds. In most parts of the middle West they are no longer seen, except in twos or threes, but once they were like the sands of the sea for multitude. It was not now the season when they hid half the heavens with their flight day after day ; but they were in myriads all through the woods, where their irides- cent breasts shone like a sudden untimely growth of flowers when you came upon them from the front. When they rose in fright, it was like the upward leap of fire, and with the roar of flame. I use images which, after all, are false to the thing I wish to ex- press; but they must serve. I tried honestly enough to kill the pigeons, but I had no luck, or too much, till I happened to bring down one of a pair that I found apart from the rest in a lofty tree-top. The poor creature I had widowed followed me to the verge of the woods, as I started home with my prey, and I

do not care to know more personally the feelings of a
murderer than I did then.   I tried to shoot the bird,
but my aim was so bad that I could not do her this
mercy, and at last she flew away, and I saw her no
more.

The spring was now opening, and I was able to
keep more and more with Nature, who was kinder to
me than I was to her other children, or wished to be,
and I got the better of my malady, which gradually
left me for no more reason apparently than it came
upon me.   But I was still far from well, and I was in
despair of my future.   I began to read again— I suppose I had really never altogether stopped.   I borrowed from my friend the bookbinder a German novel,
which had for me a message of lasting cheer.   It was
the Afraja of Theodore Mügge, a story of life in Norway during the last century, and I remember it as a
very lovely story indeed, with honest studies of character among the Norwegians, and a tender pathos in the
fate of the little Lap heroine Gula, who was perhaps
sufficiently romanced.   The hero was a young Dane,
who was going up among the fiords to seek his fortune
in the northern fisheries; and by a process inevitable
in youth I became identified with him, so that I adventured, and enjoyed, and suffered in his person

throughout. There was a supreme moment when he
was sailing through the fiords, and finding himself apparently locked in by their mountain walls without
sign or hope of escape, but somehow always escaping
by some unimagined channel, and keeping on. The
lesson for him was one of trust and courage ; and I,
who seemed to be then shut in upon a mountain-walled
fiord without inlet or outlet, took the lesson home and
promised myself not to lose heart again. It seems a
little odd that this passage of a book, by no means of
the greatest, should have had such an effect with me
at a time when I was no longer so young as to be un-
duly impressed by what I read ; but it is true that I
have never since found myself in circumstances where
there seemed to be no getting forward or going back,
without a vision of that fiord scenery, and then a rise
of faith, that if I kept on I should, somehow, come
out of my prisoning environment.

XXVI.

GEORGE ELIOT, HAWTHORNE, GOETHE, HEINE.

I GOT back health enough to be of use in the printing-office that autumn, and I was quietly at work there
with no visible break in my surroundings when suddenly the whole world opened to me through what had
seemed an impenetrable wall. The Republican newspaper at the capital had been bought by a new man-
agement, and the editorial force reorganized upon a
footing of what we then thought metropolitan enter-
prise; and to my great joy and astonishment I was
asked to come and take a place in it. The place offered me was not one of lordly distinction; in fact, it
was partly of the character of that I had already rejected in Cincinnati, but I hoped that in the smaller
city its duties would not be so odious; and by the
time I came to fill it, a change had taken place in the
arrangements so that I was given charge of the news

department. This included the literary notices and the book reviews, and I am afraid that I at once gave my prime attention to these.

It was an evening paper, and I had nearly as much time for reading and study as I had at home. But now society began to claim a share of this leisure, which I by no means begrudged it. Society was very charming in Columbus then, with a pretty constant round of dances and suppers, and an easy cordiality, which I dare say young people still find in it everywhere. I met a great many cultivated people, chiefly young ladies, and there were several houses where we young fellows went and came almost as freely as if they were our own. There we had music and cards, and talk about books, and life appeared to me richly worth living; if any one had said this was not the best planet in the universe I should have called him a pessimist, or at least thought him so, for we had not the word in those days. A world in which all those pretty and gracious women dwelt, among the figures of the waltz and the lancers, with chat between about the last installment of The Newcomes, was good enough world for me; I was only afraid it was too good. There were, of course, some girls who did not read, but few openly professed indifference to literature, and there was much lending of books back and forth, and much debate of them. That was the day when Adam Bede was a new book, and in this I had my first knowledge of that great intellect for which I had no passion, indeed, but always the deepest respect, the highest honor; and which has from time to time profoundly influenced me by its ethics.

I state these things simply and somewhat baldly; I might easily refine upon them, and study that subtle effect for good and for evil which young people are always receiving from the fiction they read; but this is not the time or place for the inquiry, and I only wish to own that so far as I understand it, the chief part of my ethical experience has been from novels. The life and character I have found portrayed there have appealed always to the consciousness of right and wrong implanted in me; and from no one has this appeal been stronger than from George Eliot. Her influence continued through many years, and I can question it now only in the undue burden she seems to throw upon the individual, and her failure to account largely enough for motive from the social environment. There her work seems to me unphilosophical.

It shares whatever error there is in its perspective

with that of Hawthorne, whose Marble Faun was a
new book at the same time that Adam Bede was new,
and whose books now came into my life and gave it
their tinge.   He was always dealing with the problem
of evil, too, and I found a more potent charm in his
more artistic handling of it than I found in George
Eliot.   Of course, I then preferred the region of pure
romance where he liked to place his action; but I did
not find his instances the less veritable because they
shone out in

> "The light that never was on sea or land."

I read the Marble Faun first, and then the Scarlet
Letter, and then the House of Seven Gables, and then
the Blithedale Romance; but I always liked best the
last, which is more nearly a novel, and more realistic
than the others.   They all moved me with a sort of
effect such as I had not felt before.   They were so far
from time and place that, although most of them related to our country and epoch, I could not imagine
anything approximate from them; and Hawthorne
himself seemed a remote and impalpable agency, rather than a person whom one might actually meet, as
not long afterward happened with me.   I did not hold
the sort of fancied converse with him that I held with
other authors, and I cannot pretend that I had the af-

fection for him that attracted me to them. But he held me by his potent spell, and for a time he dominated me as completely as any author I have read. More truly than any other American author he has been a passion with me, and lately I heard with a kind of pang a young man saying that he did not believe I should find the Scarlet Letter bear reading now. I did not assent to the possibility, but the notion gave me a shiver of dismay. I thought how much that book had been to me, how much all of Hawthorne's books had been, and to have parted with my faith in their perfection would have been something I would not willingly have risked doing.

Of course there is always something fatally weak in the scheme of the pure romance, which, after the color of the contemporary mood dies out of it, leaves it in danger of tumbling into the dust of allegory; and perhaps this inherent weakness was what that bold critic felt in the Scarlet Letter. But none of Hawthorne's fables are without a profound and distant reach into the recesses of nature and of being. He came back from his researches with no solution of the question, with no message, indeed, but the awful warning, "Be true, be true," which is the burden of the Scarlet Letter; yet in all his books there is the hue of thoughts that we think only in the presence of the mysteries of life and death.   It is not his fault that this is not intelligence, that it knots the brow in sorer doubt rather than shapes the lips to utterance of the things that can never be said.   Some of his shorter stories I have found thin and cold to my later reading, and I have never cared much for the House of Seven Gables, but the other day I was reading the Blithedale Romance again, and I found it as potent, as significant, as sadly and strangely true as when it first enthralled my soul.

In those days when I tried to kindle my heart at the cold altar of Goethe, I did read a great deal of his prose and somewhat of his poetry, but it was to be ten years yet before I should go faithfully through with his Faust and come to know its power.   For the present, I read Wilhelm Meister and the Wahlverwandschaften, and worshiped him much at second-hand through Heine.   In the meantime I invested such Germans as I met with the halo of their national poetry, and there was one lady of whom I heard with awe that she had once known my Heine.   When I came to meet her, over a glass of the mild egg-nog which she served at her house on Sunday nights, and she told me about Heine, and how he looked, and some few things he said, I suffered an indescribable disappointment; and if I could have been frank with myself I should have owned to a fear that it might have been something like that, if I had myself met the poet in the flesh, and tried to hold the intimate converse with him that I held in the spirit. But I shut my heart to all such misgivings and went on reading him much more than I read any other German author. I went on writing him too, just as I went on reading and writing Tennyson. Heine was always a personal interest with me, and every word of his made me long to have had him say it to me, and tell me why he said it. In a poet of alien race and language and religion I found a greater sympathy than I have experienced with any other. Perhaps the Jews are still the chosen people, but now they bear the message of humanity, while once they bore the message of divinity. I knew the ugliness of Heine's nature: his revengefulness, and malice, and cruelty, and treachery, and uncleanness; and yet he was supremely charming among the poets I have read. The tenderness I still feel for him is not a reasoned love, I must own; but, as I am always asking, when was love ever reasoned?

I had a room-mate that winter in Columbus who was already a contributor to the Atlantic Monthly, and who read Browning as devotedly as I read Heine.

I will not say that he wrote him as constantly, but if that had been so, I should not have cared. What I could not endure without pangs of secret jealousy was that he should like Heine, too, and should read him, though it was but at arm's-length in an English version. He had found the origins of those tricks and turns of Heine's in Tristram Shandy and the Sentimental Journey; and this galled me, as if he had shown that some mistress of my soul had studied her graces from another girl, and that it was not all her own hair that she wore. I hid my rancor as well as I could, and took what revenge lay in my power by insinuating that he might have a very different view if he read Heine in the original. I also made haste to try my own fate with the Atlantic, and I sent off to Mr. Lowell that poem which he kept so long in order to make sure that Heine had not written it, as well as authorized it.

XXVII.

CHARLES READE.

THIS was the winter when my friend Piatt and I
made our first literary venture together in those Poems
of Two Friends, which hardly passed the circle of our
amity; and it was altogether a time of high literary
exaltation with me.   I walked the streets of the
friendly little city by day and by night with my head
so full of rhymes and poetic phrases that it seemed as
if their buzzing might have been heard several yards
away; and I do not yet see quite how I contrived to
keep their music out of my newspaper paragraphs.
Out of the newspaper I could not keep it, and from
time to time I broke into verse in its columns, to the
great amusement of the leading editor, who knew me
for a young man with a very sharp tooth for such
self-betrayals in others.   He wanted to print a burlesque review he wrote of the Poems of Two Friends

in our paper, but I would not suffer it. I must allow
that it was very funny, and that he was always a generous friend, whose wounds would have been as faithful as any that could have been dealt me then. He
did not indeed care much for any poetry but that of
Shakespeare and the Ingoldsby Legends; and when
one morning a State Senator came into the office with
a volume of Tennyson, and began to read,

> " The poet in a golden clime was born,
>   With golden stars above;
>   Dowered with the hate of hate, the scorn of scorn,
>   The love of love,"

he hitched his chair about, and started in on his leader
for the day.

He might have been more patient if he had known
that this State Senator was to be President Garfield.
But who could know anything of the tragical history
that was so soon to follow that winter of 1859-60?
Not I; at least I listened rapt by the poet and the
reader, and it seemed to me as if the making and the
reading of poetry were to go on forever, and that was
to be all there was of it. To be sure I had my hard
little journalistic misgivings that it was not quite the
thing for a State Senator to come round reading Tennyson at ten o'clock in the morning, and I dare say I
felt myself superior in my point of view, though I

could not resist the charm of the verse. I myself did not bring Tennyson to the office at that time. I brought Thackeray, and I remember that one day when I had read half an hour or so in the Book of Snobs, the leading editor said frankly, Well, now, he guessed we had had enough of that. He apologized afterward as if he were to blame, and not I, but I dare say I was a nuisance with my different literary passions, and must have made many of my acquaintances very tired of my favorite authors. I had some consciousness of the fact, but I could not help it.

I ought not to omit from the list of these favorites an author who was then beginning to have his greatest vogue, and who somehow just missed of being a very great one. We were all reading his jaunty, nervy, knowing books, and some of us were questioning whether we ought not to set him above Thackeray and Dickens and George Eliot, *tutti quanti*, so great was the effect that Charles Reade had with our generation. He was a man who stood at the parting of the ways between realism and romanticism, and if he had been somewhat more of a man he might have been the master of a great school of English realism; but, as it was, he remained content to use the materials of realism and produce the effect of romanticism. He saw that life itself infinitely outvalued anything that could be feigned about it, but its richness seemed to corrupt him, and he had not the clear, ethical conscience which forced George Eliot to be realistic when probably her artistic prepossessions were romantic.

As yet, however, there was no reasoning of the matter, and Charles Reade was writing books of tremendous adventure and exaggerated character, which he prided himself on deriving from the facts of the world around him. He was intoxicated with the discovery he had made that the truth was beyond invention, but he did not know what to do with the truth in art after he had found it in life, and to this day the English mostly do not. We young people were easily taken with his glittering error, and we read him with much the same fury that he wrote. Never Too Late to Mend; Love Me Little, Love Me Long; Christie Johnstone; Peg Woffington; and then, later, Hard Cash, The Cloister and the Hearth, Foul Play, Put Yourself in His Place — how much they all meant once, or seemed to mean!

The first of them, and the other poems and fictions I was reading, meant more to me than the rumors of war that were then filling the air, and that so soon became its awful actualities. To us who have our lives

so largely in books the material world is always the
fable, and the ideal the fact. I walked with my feet
on the ground, but my head was in the clouds, as light
as any of them. I neither praise nor blame this fact;
but I feel bound to own it, for that time, and for every
time in my life, since the witchery of literature began
with me.

Those two happy winters in Columbus, when I was
finding opportunity and recognition, were the heydey
of life for me. There has been no time like them
since, though there have been smiling and prosperous
times a plenty; for then I was in the blossom of my
youth, and what I had not I could hope for without
unreason, for I had so much of that which I had most
desired. Those times passed, and there came other
times, long years of abeyance, and waiting and defeat,
which I thought would never end, but they passed,
too.

I got my appointment of Consul to Venice, and I
went home to wait for my passport and to spend the
last days, so full of civic trouble, before I should set
out for my post. If I hoped to serve my country
there and sweep the Confederate cruisers from the
Adriatic, I am afraid my prime intent was to add to
her literature and to my own credit. I intended,

while keeping a sleepless eye out for privateers, to write poems concerning American life which should eclipse anything yet done in that kind, and in the meantime I read voraciously and perpetually, to make the days go swiftly which I should have been so glad to have linger. In this month I devoured all the Waverley novels, but I must have been devouring a great many others, for Charles Reade's Christie Johnstone is associated with the last moment of the last days.

A few months ago I was at the old home, and I read that book again, after not looking at it for more than thirty years; and I read it with amazement at its prevailing artistic vulgarity, its prevailing æsthetic error shot here and there with gleams of light, and of the truth that Reade himself was always dimly groping for. The book is written throughout on the verge of realism, with divinations and conjectures across its border, and with lapses into the fool's paradise of romanticism, and an apparent content with its inanity and impossibility. But then it was brilliantly new and surprising; it seemed to be the last word that could be said for the truth in fiction; and it had a spell that held us like an anæsthetic above the ache of parting, and the anxiety for the years that must pass, with all their redoubled chances, before our home circle could be made whole again.   I read on, and the rest listened, till the wheels of the old stage made themselves heard in their approach through the absolute silence of the village street.   Then we shut the book and all went down to the gate together, and parted under the pale sky of the October night.   There was one of the home group whom I was not to see again : the young brother who died in the blossom of his years before I returned from my far and strange sojourn.   He was too young then to share our reading of the novel, but when I ran up to his room to bid him good-by I found him awake, and, with aching hearts, we bade each other good-by forever !

XXVIII.

DANTE.

I RAN through an Italian grammar on my way across the Atlantic, and from my knowledge of Latin, Spanish and French, I soon had a reading acquaintance with the language. I had really wanted to go to Germany, that I might carry forward my studies in German literature, and I first applied for the consulate at Munich. The powers at Washington thought it quite the same thing to offer me Rome; but I found that the income of the Roman consulate would not give me a living, and I was forced to decline it. Then the President's private secretaries, Mr. John Nicolay and Mr. John Hay, who did not know me except as a young Westerner who had written poems in the Atlantic Monthly, asked me how I would like Venice, and promised that they would have the salary put up to a thousand a year, under the new law to embarrass privateers. It was really put up to fifteen hundred, and with this income assured to me I went out to the city whose influence changed the whole course of my literary life.

No privateers ever came, though I once had notice from Turin that the Florida had been sighted off Ancona; and I had nearly four years of nearly uninterrupted leisure at Venice, which I meant to employ in reading all Italian literature, and writing a history of the republic. The history, of course, I expected would be a long affair, and I did not quite suppose that I could dispatch the literature in any short time; besides, I had several considerable poems on hand that occupied me a good deal, and I worked at these as well as advanced myself in Italian, preparatory to the efforts before me.

I had already a fairish general notion of Italian letters from Leigh Hunt, and from other agreeable English Italianates; and I knew that I wanted to read not only the four great poets, Dante, Petrarch, Ariosto and Tasso, but that whole group of burlesque poets, Pulci, Berni, and the rest, who, from what I knew of them, I thought would be even more to my mind. As a matter of fact, and in the process of time, I did read somewhat of all these, but rather in the minor than

the major way ; and I soon went off from them to the
study of the modern poets, novelists and playwrights
who interested me so much more.   After my wonted
fashion I read half a dozen of these authors together,
so that it would be hard to say which I began with,
but I had really a devotion to Dante, though not at
that time, or ever for the whole of Dante.   During
my first year in Venice I met an ingenious priest, who
had been a tutor in a patrician family, and who was
willing to lead my faltering steps through the Inferno.
This part of the Divine Comedy I read with a begin-
ner's carefulness, and with a rapture in its beauties,
which I will whisper the reader do not appear in every
line.

Again I say it is a great pity that criticism is not
honest about the masterpieces of literature, and does
not confess that they are not every moment masterly,
that they are often dull and tough and dry, as is certainly the case with Dante's.   Some day, perhaps, we
shall have this way of treating literature, and then the
lover of it will not feel obliged to browbeat himself
into the belief that if he is not always enjoying himself it is his own fault.   At any rate I will permit
myself the luxury of frankly saying that while I had
a deep sense of the majesty and grandeur of Dante's

design, many points of its execution bored me, and
that I found the intermixture of small local fact and
neighborhood history in the fabric of his lofty creation
no part of its noblest effect. What is marvelous in
it is its expression of Dante's personality, and I can
never think that his personalities enhance its greatness
as a work of art. I enjoyed them, however, and I
enjoyed them the more, as the innumerable perspectives of Italian history began to open all about me.
Then, indeed, I understood the origins if I did not
understand the aims of Dante, which there is still
much dispute about among those who profess to know
them clearly. What I finally perceived was that his
poem came through him from the heart of Italian life,
such as it was in his time, and that whatever it
teaches, his poem expresses that life, in all its splendor and squalor, its beauty and deformity, its love and
its hate.

Criticism may torment this sense or that sense out
of it, but at the end of the ends the Divine Comedy
will stand for the patriotism of mediæval Italy, as far
as its ethics is concerned, and for a profound and lofty
ideal of beauty, as far as its æsthetics is concerned.
This is vague enough and slight enough, I must confess, but I must confess also that I had not even a

conception of so much when I first read the Inferno.
I went at it very simply, and my enjoyment of it was
that sort which finds its account in the fine passages,
the brilliant episodes, the striking pictures. This was
the effect with me of all the criticism which I had
hitherto read, and I am not sure yet that the criticism
which tries to be of a larger scope, and to see things
"whole," is of any definite effect. As a matter of
fact we see nothing whole, neither life nor art. We
are so made, in soul and in sense, that we can deal
only with parts, with points, with degrees; and the
endeavor to compass any entirety must involve a dis-
comfort and a danger very threatening to our intellectual integrity.

Or if this postulate is as untenable as all the others,
still I am very glad that I did not then lose any fact
of the majesty, and beauty, and pathos of the great
certain measures for the sake of that fourth dimension
of the poem which is not yet made palpable or visible.
I took my sad heart's fill of the sad story of Paolo and
Francesca, which I already knew in Leigh Hunt's
adorable dilution, and most of the lines read themselves into my memory, where they linger yet. I
supped on the horrors of Ugolino's fate with the
strong gust of youth, which finds every exercise of

sympathy a pleasure. My good priest sat beside me in these rich moments, knotting in his lap the calico handkerchief of the snuff-taker, and entering with tremulous eagerness into my joy in things that he had often before enjoyed. No doubt he had an inexhaustible pleasure in them apart from mine, for I have found my pleasure in them perennial, and have not failed to taste it as often as I have read or repeated any of the great passages of the poem to myself. This pleasure came often from some vital phrase, or merely the inspired music of a phrase quite apart from its meaning. I did not get then, and I have not got since, a distinct conception of the journey through Hell, and as often as I have tried to understand the topography of the poem I have fatigued myself to no purpose, but I do not think the essential meaning was lost upon me.

I dare say my priest had his notion of the general shape and purport, the gross material body of the thing, but he did not trouble me with it, while we sat tranced together in the presence of its soul. He seemed, at times, so lost in the beatific vision, that he forgot my stumblings in the philological darkness, till I appealed to him for help. Then he would read aloud with that magnificent rhythm the Italians have

in reading their verse, and the obscured meaning
would seem to shine out of the mere music of the
poem, like the color the blind feel in sound.

I do not know what has become of him, but if he
is like the rest of the strange group of my guides,
philosophers, and friends in literature—the printer,
the organ-builder, the machinist, the drug-clerk and
the bookbinder—I am afraid he is dead. In fact, I
who was then I, might be said to be dead too, so little
is my past self like my present self in anything but
the "increasing purpose" which has kept me one in
my love of literature. He was a gentle and kindly
man, with a life and a longing, quite apart from his
vocation, which were never lived or fulfilled. I did
not see him after he ceased to read Dante with me,
and in fact I was instructed by the suspicions of my
Italian friends to be careful how I consorted with a
priest, who might very well be an Austrian spy. I
parted with him for no such picturesque reason, for I
never believed him other than the truest and faithful-
est of friends, but because I was then giving myself
more entirely to work in which he could not help me.

Naturally enough this was a long poem in the *terza
rima* of the Divina Commedia, and dealing with a
story of our civil war in a fashion so remote that no

editor would print it. This was the first fruits and
the last of my reading of Dante, in verse, and it was
not so like Dante as I would have liked to make it;
but Dante is not easy to imitate; he is too unconscious,
and too single, too bent upon saying the thing that is
in him, with whatever beauty inheres in it, to put on
the graces that others may catch.

XXIX.

GOLDONI, MANZONI, D'AZEGLIO.

HOWEVER, this poem only shared the fate of nearly all the others that I wrote at this time; they came back to me with unfailing regularity from all the magazine editors of the English-speaking world; I had no success with any of them till I sent Mr. Lowell a paper on recent Italian comedy for the North American Review, which he and Professor Norton had then begun to edit. I was in the meantime printing the material of Venetian Life and the Italian Journeys in a Boston newspaper after its rejection by the magazines; and my literary life, almost without my willing it, had taken the course of critical observance of books and men in their actuality.

That is to say, I was studying manners, in the elder sense of the word, wherever I could get at them in the frank life of the people about me, and in such

literature of Italy as was then modern.   In this pursuit I made a discovery that greatly interested me,
and that specialized my inquiries.   I found that the
Italians had no novels which treated of their contemporary life; that they had no modern fiction but the
historical romance.   I found that if I wished to know
their life from their literature I must go to their drama, which was even then endeavoring to give their
stage a faithful picture of their civilization.   There was
even then, in the new circumstance of a people just
liberated from every variety of intellectual repression
and political oppression, a group of dramatic authors,
whose plays were not only delightful to see but delightful to read, working in the good tradition of one
of the greatest realists who has ever lived, and pro-
ducing a drama of vital strength and charm.   One of
them, whom I by no means thought the best, has given
us a play, known to all the world, which I am almost
ready to think with Zola is the greatest play of modern times; or if it is not so, I should be puzzled to
name the modern drama that surpasses La Morte Civile of Paolo Giacometti.   I learned to know all the
dramatists pretty well, in the whole range of their
work, on the stage and in the closet, and I learned to
know still better, and to love supremely, the fine, ami-

able genius whom, as one of them said, they did not
so much imitate as learn from to imitate nature.

This was Carlo Goldoni, the first of the realists, but
antedating conscious realism so long as to have been
born at Venice early in the eighteenth century, and to
have come to his hand-to-hand fight with the romanticism of his day almost before that century had
reached its noon. In the early sixties of our own century I was no more conscious of his realism than he
was himself a hundred years before; but I had eyes
in my head, and I saw that what he had seen in Venice so long before was so true that it was the very life
of Venice in my own day; and because I have loved
the truth in art above all other things, I fell instantly
and lastingly in love with Carlo Goldoni. I was reading his memoirs, and learning to know his sweet, honest, simple nature while I was learning to know his
work, and I wish that every one who reads his plays
would read his life as well; one must know him before one can fully know them. I believe, in fact, that
his autobiography came into my hands first. But, at
any rate, both are associated with the fervors and lan-
guors of that first summer in Venice, so that I cannot
take up a book of Goldoni's without a renewed sense
of that sunlight and moonlight, and of the sounds and

silences of a city that is at once the stillest and shrillest in the world.

Perhaps because I never found his work of great ethical or æsthetical proportions, but recognized that it pretended to be good only within its strict limitations, I recur to it now without that painful feeling of a diminished grandeur in it, which attends us so often when we go back to something that once greatly pleased us. It seemed to me at the time that I must have read all his comedies in Venice, but I kept reading new ones after I came home, and still I can take a volume of his from the shelf, and when thirty years are past, find a play or two that I missed before. Their number is very great, but perhaps those that I fancy I have not read, I have really read once or more and forgotten. That might very easily be, for there is seldom anything more poignant in any one of them than there is in the average course of things. The plays are light and amusing transcripts from life, for the most part, and where at times they deepen into powerful situations, or express strong emotions, they do so with persons so little different from the average of our acquaintance that we do not remember just who the persons are.

There is no doubt but the kindly playwright had

his conscience, and meant to make people think as well as laugh. I know of none of his plays that is of wrong effect, or that violates the instincts of purity, or insults common sense with the romantic pretense that wrong will be right if you will only paint it rose-color. He is at some obvious pains to "punish vice and reward virtue," but I do not mean that easy morality when I praise his; I mean the more difficult sort that recognizes in each man's soul the arbiter not of his fate surely, but surely of his peace. He never makes a fool of the spectator by feigning that passion is a reason or justification, or that suffering of one kind can atone for wrong of another. That was left for the romanticists of our own century to discover; even the romanticists whom Goldoni drove from the stage, were of that simpler eighteenth-century sort who had not yet liberated the individual from society, but held him accountable in the old way. As for Goldoni himself, he apparently never dreams of transgression; he is of rather an explicit conventionality in most things, and he deals with society as something finally settled. How artfully he deals with it, how decently, how wholesomely, those who know Venetian society of the eighteenth century historically will perceive when they recall the adequate impression he gives of it without offense in character or language or situation. This is the perpetual miracle of his comedy, that it says so much to experience and worldly wisdom, and so little to inexperience and worldly innocence. No doubt the Serenest Republic was very strict with the theatre, and suffered it to hold the mirror up to nature only when nature was behaving well, or at least behaving as if young people were present. Yet the Italians are rather plain-spoken, and they recognize facts which our company manners at least do not admit the existence of. I should say that Goldoni was almost English, almost American, indeed, in his observance of the proprieties, and I like this in him; though the proprieties are not virtues, they are very good things, and at least are better than the improprieties.

This, however, I must own, had not a great deal to do with my liking him so much, and I should be puzzled to account for my passion, as much in his case as in most others. If there was any reason for it, perhaps it was that he had the power of taking me out of my life, and putting me into the lives of others, whom I felt to be human beings as much as myself. To make one live in others, this is the highest effect of religion as well as of art, and possibly it will be the highest bliss we shall ever know. I do not pretend that my translation was through my unselfishness; it was distinctly through that selfishness which perceives that self is misery; and I may as well confess here that I do not regard the artistic ecstasy as in any sort noble. It is not noble to love the beautiful, or to live for it, or by it; and it may even not be refining. I would not have any reader of mine, looking forward to some æsthetic career, suppose that this love is any merit in itself; it may be the grossest egotism. If you cannot look beyond the end you aim at, and seek the good which is not your own, all your sacrifice is to yourself and not of yourself, and you might as well be going into business. In itself and for itself it is no more honorable to win fame than to make money, and the wish to do the one is no more elevating than the wish to do the other.

But in the days I write of I had no conception of this, and I am sure that my blindness to so plain a fact kept me even from seeking and knowing the highest beauty in the things I worshiped. I believe that if I had been sensible of it I should have read much more of such humane Italian poets and novelists as Manzoni and D'Azeglio, whom I perceived to be delightful, without dreaming of them in the length and breadth of their goodness. Now and then its extent flashed upon me, but the glimpse was lost to my retroverted vision almost as soon as won. It is only in thinking back to them that I can realize how much they might always have meant to me. They were both living in my time in Italy, and they were two men whom I should now like very much to have seen, if I could have done so without that futility which seems to attend every effort to pay one's duty to such men.

The love of country in all the Italian poets and romancers of the long period of the national resurrection ennobled their art in a measure which criticism has not yet taken account of. I conceived of its effect then, but I conceived of it as a misfortune, a fatality; now I am by no means sure that it was so; hereafter the creation of beauty, as we call it, for beauty's sake, may be considered something monstrous. There is forever a poignant meaning in life beyond what mere living involves, and why should not there be this reference in art to the ends beyond art? The situation, the long patience, the hope against hope, dignified and beautified the nature of the Italian writers of that day, and evoked from them a quality which I was too little trained in their school to appreciate. But in a sort I did feel it, I did know it in them all, so far as I knew any of them, and in the tragedies of Manzoni, and in the romances of D'Azeglio, and yet more in the simple and modest records of D'Azeglio's life published after his death, I profited by it, and unconsciously prepared myself for that point of view whence all the arts appear one with all the uses, and there is nothing beautiful that is false.

I am very glad of that experience of Italian literature, which I look back upon as altogether wholesome and sanative, after my excesses of Heine. No doubt it was all a minor affair as compared with equal knowledge of French literature, and so far it was a loss of time. It is idle to dispute the general positions of criticism, and there is no useful gainsaying its judgment that French literature is a major literature and Italian a minor literature in this century; but whether this verdict will stand for all time, there may be a reasonable doubt. Criterions may change, and hereafter people may look at the whole affair so differently that a literature which went to the making of a people will not be accounted a minor literature, but will take its place with the great literary movements.

I do not insist upon this possibility, and I am far from defending myself for liking the comedies of

Goldoni better than the comedies of Molière, upon purely æsthetic grounds, where there is no question as to the artistic quality.   Perhaps it is because I came to Molière's comedies later, and with my taste formed for those of Goldoni; but again, it is here a matter of affection; I find Goldoni for me more sympathetic, and because he is more sympathetic I cannot do otherwise than find him more natural, more true.   I will allow that this is vulnerable, and as I say, I do not defend it.   Molière has a place in literature infinitely loftier than Goldoni's; and he has supplied types, characters, phrases, to the currency of thought, and Goldoni has supplied none.   It is, therefore, without reason which I can allege that I enjoy Goldoni more.   I am perfectly willing to be rated low for my preference, and yet I think that if it had been Goldoni's luck to have had the great age of a mighty monarchy for his scene, instead of the decline of an outworn republic, his place in literature might have been different.

XXX.

PASTOR FIDO, AMINTA, ROMOLA, YEAST, PAUL FERROLL.

But I have always had a great love for the absolutely unreal, the purely fanciful in all the arts, as well as of the absolutely real ; I like the one on a far lower plane than the other, but it delights me, as a pantomime at a theatre does, or a comic opera, which has its being wholly outside the realm of the probabilities. When I once transport myself to this sphere I have no longer any care for them, and if I could I would not exact of them an allegiance which has no concern with them. For this reason I have always vastly enjoyed the artificialities of pastoral poetry ; and in Venice I read with a pleasure few serious poems have given me the Pastor Fido of Guarini. I came later but not with fainter zest to the Aminta of Tasso, without which, perhaps, the Pastor Fido would not have been, and I reveled in the pretty impossibilities of both these charming effects of the liberated imagination.

I do not the least condemn that sort of thing; one does not live by sweets, unless one is willing to spoil one's teeth and digestion; but one may now and then indulge one's self without harm, and a sugar plum or two after dinner may even be of advantage. What I object to is the romantic thing which asks to be accepted with all its fantasticality on the ground of reality; that seems to me hopelessly bad. But I have been able to dwell in their charming out-land or no-land with the shepherds and shepherdesses and nymphs, satyrs and fauns, of Tasso and Guarini, and I take the finest pleasure in their company, their Dresden china loves and sorrows, their airy raptures, their painless throes, their polite anguish, their tears not the least salt, but flowing as sweet as the purling streams of their enameled meadows. I wish there were more of that sort of writing; I should like very much to read it.

The greater part of my reading in Venice, when I began to find that I could not help writing about the place, was in books relating to its life and history, which I made use of rather than found pleasure in. My studies in Italian literature were full of the most charming interest, and if I had to read a good many books for conscience' sake, there were a good many others I read for their own sake. They were chiefly poetry; and after the first essays in which I tasted the classic poets, they were chiefly the books of the modern poets.

For the present I went no farther in German literature, and I recurred to it in later years only for deeper and fuller knowledge of Heine; my Spanish was ignored, as all first loves are when one has reached the age of twenty-six. My English reading was almost wholly in the Tauchnitz editions, for otherwise English books were not easily come at then and there. George Eliot's Romola was then new, and I read it again and again with the sense of moral enlargement which the first fiction to conceive of the true nature of evil gave all of us who were young in that day. Tito Malemma was not only a lesson, he was a revelation, and I trembled before him as in the presence of a warning and a message from the only veritable perdition. His life, in which so much that was good was mixed with so much that was bad, lighted up the whole domain of egotism with its glare, and made one feel how near the best and the worst were to each other, and how they sometimes touched without absolute di-

vision in texture and color. The book was undoubtedly
a favorite of mine, and I did not see then the artistic
falterings in it which were afterward evident to me.

There were not Romolas to read all the time,
though, and I had to devolve upon inferior authors for
my fiction the greater part of the time.   Of course, I
kept up with Our Mutual Friend, which Dickens was
then writing, and with Philip, which was to be the
last of Thackeray.   I was not yet sufficiently instructed
to appreciate Trollope, and I did not read him at all.

I got hold of Kingsley, and read Yeast, and I think
some other novels of his, with great relish, and without sensibility to his Charles Readeish lapses from his
art into the material of his art.   But of all the minor
fiction that I read at this time none impressed me so
much as three books which had then already had their
vogue, and which I knew somewhat from reviews.
They were Paul Ferroll, Why Paul Ferroll killed his
Wife, and Day after Day.   The first two were, of
course, related to each other, and they were all three
full of unwholesome force.   As to their æsthetic merit
I will not say anything, for I have not looked at either
of the books for thirty years.   I fancy, however, that
their strength was rather of the tetanic than the titanic
sort.   They made your sympathies go with the hero,

who deliberately puts his wife to death for the lie she told to break off his marriage with the woman he had loved, and who then marries this tender and gentle girl, and lives in great happiness with her till her death. Murder in the first degree is flattered by his fate up to the point of letting him die peacefully in Boston after these dealings of his in England; and altogether his story could not be commended to people with a morbid taste for bloodshed. Naturally enough the books were written by a perfectly good woman, the wife of an English clergyman, whose friends were greatly scandalized by them. As a sort of atonement she wrote Day after Day, the story of a dismal and joyless orphan, who dies to the sound of angelic music, faint and far-heard, filling the whole chamber. A carefuller study of the phenomenon reveals the fact that the seraphic strains are produced by the steam escaping from the hot-water bottles at the feet of the invalid.

As usual, I am not able fully to account for my liking of these books, and I am so far from wishing to justify it that I think I ought rather to excuse it. But since I was really greatly fascinated with them, and read them with an ever-growing fascination, the only honest thing to do is to own my subjection to them. It would be an interesting and important question for criticism to study, that question why certain books at a certain time greatly dominate our fancy, and others manifestly better have no influence with us. A curious proof of the subtlety of these Paul Ferroll books in the appeal they made to the imagination is the fact that I came to them fresh from Romola, and full of horror for myself in Tito; yet I sympathized throughout with Paul Ferroll, and was glad when he got away.

XXXI.

ON my return to America, my literary life immediately took such form that most of my reading was
done for review. I wrote at first a good many of the
lighter criticisms in The Nation, at New York, and
after I went to Boston to become the assistant editor
of the Atlantic Monthly I wrote the literary notices in
that periodical for four or five years.

It was only when I came into full charge of the
magazine that I began to share these labors with others, and I continued them in some measure as long as
I had any relation to it. My reading for reading's
sake, as I had hitherto done it, was at an end, and I
read primarily for the sake of writing about the book
in hand, and secondarily for the pleasure it might
give me. This was always considerable, and sometimes so great that I forgot the critic in it, and read

on and on for pleasure. I was master to review this book or that as I chose, and generally I reviewed only books I liked to read, though sometimes I felt that I ought to do a book, and did it from a sense of duty; these perfunctory criticisms I do not think were very useful, but I tried to make them honest.

Among the first books that came to my hand was a novel of J. W. De Forest, which I think the best novel suggested by the civil war. If this is not saying very much for Miss Ravenel's Conversion, I will go farther and say it was one of the best American novels that I had known, and was of an advanced realism, before realism was known by name. I had a passion for that book, and for all the books of that author; and if I have never been able to make the public care for them as much as I did it has not been for want of trying. Kate Beaumont, Honest John Vane, Playing the Mischief, are admirable fictions, sprung from our own life, of strong fibre and firm growth; all that Mr. De Forest has written is of a texture and color distinctly his own; his short stories are as good as his long ones. I have thought it more discreditable to our taste than to his talent that he has not been recognized as one of our foremost novelists, for his keen and accurate touch in character, his wide scope, and his unerring rendition of whatever he has attempted to report of American life; but I do not know that I shall ever persuade either critics or readers to think with me.

At the same time that I made the acquaintance of this writer I came to a knowledge of Mr. Henry James's wonderful workmanship in the first manuscript of his that passed through my hands as a sub-editor. I fell in love with it instantly, and I have never ceased to delight in that exquisite artistry. I have read all that he has written, and I have never read anything of his without an ecstatic pleasure in his unrivaled touch. In literary handling no one who has written fiction in our language can approach him, and his work has shown an ever-deepening insight. I have my reserves in regard to certain things of his; if hard pressed I might even undertake to better him here and there, but after I had done that I doubt if I should like him so well. In fact, I prefer to let him alone, to take him for what he is in himself, and to be grateful for every new thing that comes from his pen. I will not try to say why his works take me so much; that is no part of my business in these papers, and I can understand why other people are not taken at all with him, for no reason that they can give, either. At the same time,

I have no patience with them, and but small regard
for their taste.

In a long sickness, which I had shortly after I went
to live in Cambridge, a friend brought me several of
the stories of Erckmann-Chatrian, whom people were
then reading much more than they are now, I believe;
and I had a great joy in them, which I have renewed
since as often as I have read one of their books. They
have much the same quality of simple and sincerely
moralized realism that I found afterward in the work
of the early Swiss realist, Jeremias Gotthelf, and very
likely it was this that captivated my judgment. As
for my affections, battered and exhausted as they
ought to have been in many literary passions, they
never went out with fresher enjoyment than they did
to the charming story of L'Ami Fritz, which, when I
merely name it, breathes the spring sun and air about
me, and fills my senses with the beauty and sweetness
of cherry blossoms. It is a lovely book, one of the
loveliest and kindest that ever was written, and my
heart belongs to it still; to be sure it belongs to several hundreds of other books in equal entirety.

It belongs to all the books of the great Norwegian
Björstjerne Björnson, whose Arne, and whose Happy
Boy, and whose Fisher Maiden I read in this same for-

tunate sickness. I have since read every other book
of his that I could lay hands on: Sinnöve Solbakken,
and Magnhild, and Captain Manzana, and Dust, and
In God's Ways, and Sigurd, and plays like The Glove
and The Bankrupt. He has never, as some authors
have, dwindled in my sense; when I open his page,
there I find him as large, and free and bold as ever.
He is a great talent, a clear conscience, a beautiful
art. He has my love not only because he is a poet of
the most exquisite verity, but because he is a lover of
men, with a faith in them such as can move mount-
ains of ignorance, and dullness, and greed. He is next
to Tolstoy in his willingness to give himself for his
kind; if he would rather give himself in fighting than
in suffering wrong, I do not know that his self-sacri-
fice is less in degree.

I confess, however, that I do not think of him as a
patriot and a socialist when I read him; he is then
purely a poet, whose gift holds me rapt above the
world where I have left my troublesome and weari-
some self for the time. I do not know of any novels
that a young endeavorer in fiction could more profit-
ably read than his for their large and simple method,
their trust of the reader's intelligence, their sympathy
with life. With him the problems are all soluble by

the enlightened and regenerate will; there is no baf-
fling Fate, but a helping God.   In Björnson there is
nothing of Ibsen's scornful despair, nothing of his an-
archistic contempt, but his art is full of the warmth
and color of a poetic soul, with no touch of the icy
cynicism which freezes you in the other.   I have felt
the cold fascination of Ibsen, too, and I should be far
from denying his mighty mastery, but he has never
possessed me with the delight that Björnson has.

In those days I read not only all the new books, but
I made many forays into the past, and came back now
and then with rich spoil, though I confess that for the
most part I had my trouble for my pains; and I wish
now that I had given the time I spent on the English
classics to contemporary literature, which I have not
the least hesitation in saying I like vastly better.   In
fact, I believe that the preference for the literature of
the past, except in the case of the greatest masters, is
mainly the affectation of people who cannot otherwise
distinguish themselves from the herd, and who wish
very much to do so.

There is much to be learned from the minor novelists and poets of the past about people's ways of
thinking and feeling, but not much that the masters
do not give you in better quality and fuller measure;

and I should say, Read the old masters and let their schools go, rather than neglect any possible master of your own time. Above all, I would not have any one read an old author merely that he might not be ignorant of him; that is most beggarly, and no good can come of it. When literature becomes a duty it ceases to be a passion, and all the schoolmastering in the world, solemnly addressed to the conscience, cannot make the fact otherwise. It is well to read for the sake of knowing a certain ground if you are to make use of your knowledge in a certain way, but it would be a mistake to suppose that this is a love of literature.

XXXII.

TOURGUENIEF, AUERBACH.

In those years at Cambridge my most notable literary experience without doubt was the knowledge of
Tourguenief's novels, which began to be recognized
in all their greatness about the middle seventies. I
think they made their way with such of our public as
were able to appreciate them before they were accepted in England; but that does not matter. It is
enough for the present purpose that Smoke, and Lisa,
and On the Eve, and Dimitri Roudine, and Spring
Floods, passed one after another through my hands,
and that I formed for their author one of the pro-
foundest literary passions of my life.

I now think that there is a finer and truer method
than his, but in its way, Tourguenief's method is as
far as art can go. That is to say, his fiction is to the
last degree dramatic. The persons are sparely de-
scribed, and briefly accounted for, and then they are
left to transact their affair, whatever it is, with the
least possible comment or explanation from the author.
The effect flows naturally from their characters, and

when they have done or said a thing you conjecture
why as unerringly as you would if they were people
whom you knew outside of a book. I had already
conceived of the possibility of this from Björnson,
who practices the same method, but I was still too
sunken in the gross darkness of English fiction to rise
to a full consciousness of its excellence.   When I remembered the deliberate and impertinent moralizing
of Thackeray, the clumsy exegesis of George Eliot, the
knowing nods and winks of Charles Reade, the stage-
carpentering and lime-lighting of Dickens, even the
fine and important analysis of Hawthorne, it was with
a joyful astonishment that I realized the great art of
Tourguenief.

Here was a master who was apparently not trying
to work out a plot, who was not even trying to work
out a character, but was standing aside from the whole
affair, and letting the characters work the plot out.
The method was revealed perfectly in Smoke, but each
successive book of his that I read was a fresh proof of
its truth, a revelation of its transcendent superiority.
I think now that I exaggerated its value somewhat;
but this was inevitable in the first surprise.   The sane
æsthetics of the first Russian author I read, however,
have seemed more and more an essential part of the

sane ethics of all the Russians I have read. It was
not only that Tourguenief had painted life truly, but
that he had painted it conscientiously.

Tourguenief was of that great race which has more
than any other fully and freely uttered human nature,
without either false pride or false shame in its naked-
ness. His themes were oftenest those of the French
novelist, but how far he was from handling them in
the French manner and with the French spirit! In his
hands sin suffered no dramatic punishment; it did not
always show itself as unhappiness, in the personal
sense, but it was always unrest, and without the hope
of peace. If the end did not appear, the fact that it
must be miserable always appeared. Life showed itself to me in different colors after I had once read
Tourguenief; it became more serious, more awful, and
with mystical responsibilities I had not known before.
My gay American horizons were bathed in the vast
melancholy of the Slav, patient, agnostic, trustful. At
the same time nature revealed herself to me through
him with an intimacy she had not hitherto shown me.
There are passages in this wonderful writer alive with
a truth that seems drawn from the reader's own knowledge: who else but Tourguenief and one's own most
secret self ever felt all the rich, sad meaning of the

night air drawing in at the open window, of the fires
burning in the darkness on the distant fields? I try
in vain to give some notion of the subtle sympathy
with nature which scarcely put itself into words with
him. As for the people of his fiction, though they
were of orders and civilizations so remote from my
experience, they were of the eternal human types
whose origin and potentialities every one may find in
his own heart, and I felt their verity in every touch.

I cannot describe the satisfaction his work gave me;
I can only impart some sense of it, perhaps, by saying
that it was like a happiness I had been waiting for all
my life, and now that it had come, I was richly content forever. I do not mean to say that the art of
Tourguenief surpasses the art of Björnson; I think
Björnson is quite as fine and true. But the Norwegian deals with simple and primitive circumstances for
the most part, and always with a small world; and the
Russian has to do with human nature inside of its
conventional shells, and his scene is often as large as
Europe. Even when it is as remote as Norway, it is
still related to the great capitals by the history if not
the actuality of the characters. Most of Tourguenief's
books I have read many times over, all of them I have
read more than twice. For a number of years I read

them again and again without much caring for other fiction. It was only the other day that I read Smoke through once more, with no diminished sense of its truth, but with somewhat less than my first satisfaction in its art. Perhaps this was because I had reached the point through my acquaintance with Tolstoy where I was impatient even of the artifice that hid itself. In Smoke I was now aware of an artifice that kept out of sight, but was still always present somewhere, invisibly operating the story.

I must not fail to own the great pleasure that I have had in some of the stories of Auerbach. It is true that I have never cared greatly for On the Heights, which in its dealing with royalties seems too far aloof from the ordinary human life, and which on the moral side finally fades out into a German mistiness. But I speak of it with the imperfect knowledge of one who was never able to read it quite through, and I have really no right to speak of it. The book of his that pleased me most was Edelweiss, which, though the story was somewhat too catastrophical, seemed to me admirably good and true. I still think it very delicately done, and with a deep insight; but there is something in all Auerbach's work which in the retrospect affects me as if it dealt with pigmies.

XXXIII.

CERTAIN PREFERENCES AND EXPERIENCES.

I HAVE always loved history, whether in the annals of peoples or in the lives of persons, and I have at all times read it. I am not sure but I rather prefer it to fiction, though I am aware that in looking back over this record of my literary passions I must seem to have cared for very little besides fiction. I read at the time I have just been speaking of, nearly all the new poetry as it came out, and I constantly recurred to it in its mossier sources, where it sprang from the green English ground, or trickled from the antique urns of Italy.

I do not think that I have ever cared much for metaphysics, or to read much in that way, but from time to time I have done something of it.

Travels, of course, I have read as part of the great human story, and autobiography has at times appeared to me the most delightful reading in the world ; I have a taste in it that rejects nothing, though I have never enjoyed any autobiographies so much as those of such Italians as have reasoned of themselves.

I suppose I have not been a great reader of the drama, and I do not know that I have ever greatly relished any plays but those of Shakespeare and Goldoni, and two or three of Beaumont and Fletcher, and one or so of Marlow's, and all of Ibsen's and Maeterlinck's. The taste for the old English dramatists I believe I have never formed.

Criticism, ever since I filled myself so full of it in my boyhood, I have not cared for, and often I have found it repulsive.

I have a fondness for books of popular science, perhaps because they too are part of the human story.

I have read somewhat of the theology of the Swedenborgian faith I was brought up in, but I have not read other theological works; and I do not apologize for not liking any. The Bible itself was not much known to me at an age when most children have been obliged to read it several times over; the gospels were indeed familiar, and they have always been to me the supreme human story; but the rest of the New Testament I had not read when a man grown, and only passages of the Old Testament, like the story of the Creation, and the story of Joseph, and the poems of Job and Ecclesiastes, with occasional Psalms. I therefore came to the Scriptures with a sense at once fresh and mature, and I can never be too glad that I learned to see them under the vaster horizon and in the truer perspectives of experience.

Again as lights on the human story I have liked to read such books of medicine as have fallen in my way, and I seldom take up a medical periodical without reading of all the cases it describes, and in fact every article in it.

But I did not mean to make even this slight departure from the main business of these papers, which is to confide my literary passions to the reader; he probably has had a great many of his own. I think I may class the Ring and the Book among them, though I have never been otherwise a devotee of Browning. But I was still newly home from Italy, or away from home, when that poem appeared, and whether or not it was because it took me so with the old enchantment of that land, I gave my heart promptly to it. Of course, there are terrible *longueurs* in it, and you do get tired of the same story told over and over from the different points of view, and yet it is such a great story, and unfolded with such a magnificent breadth and noble fullness, that one who blames it lightly blames himself heavily. There are certain books of it — Caponsacchi's story, Pompilia's story, and Count Guido's story — that I think ought to rank with the greatest poetry ever written, and that have a direct, dramatic expression of the fact and character, which is without rival. There is a noble and lofty pathos in the close of Caponsacchi's statement, an artless and manly break from his self-control throughout, that seems to me the last possible effect in its kind; and Pompilia's story holds all of womanhood in it, the purity, the passion, the tenderness, the helplessness. But if I begin to praise this or any of the things I have liked, I do not know when I should stop. Yes, as I think it over, the Ring and the Book appears to me one of the great few poems whose splendor can never suffer lasting eclipse, however it may have presently fallen into abeyance. If it had impossibly come down to us from some elder time, or had not been so perfectly modern in its recognition of feeling and motives ignored by the less conscious poetry of the past, it would be ranked where it belongs, with the great epics.

Of other modern poets I have read some things of

William Morris, like the Life and Death of Jason, the
Story of Gudrun, and the Trial of Guinevere, with a
pleasure little less than passionate, and I have equally
liked certain pieces of Dante Rossetti. I have had a
high joy in some of the great minor poems of Emerson, where the goddess moves over Concord meadows
with a gait that is Greek, and her sandaled tread expresses a high scorn of the india-rubber boots that the
American muse so often gets about in.

The Commemoration Ode of Lowell has also been
a source from which I drank something of the divine
ecstasy of the poet's own exalted mood, and I would
set this level with the Bigelow Papers, high above all
his other work, and chief of the things this age of our
country shall be remembered by. Holmes I always
loved, and not for his wit alone, which is so obvious
to liking, but for those rarer and richer strains of his
in which he shows himself the lover of nature and the
brother of men. The deep spiritual insight, the celes-
tial music, and the brooding tenderness of Whittier
have always taken me more than his fierier appeals
and his civic virtues, though I do not underrate the
value of these in his verse.

My acquaintance with these modern poets, and many
I do not name because they are so many, has been

continuous with their work, and my pleasure in it not inconstant if not equal. I have spoken before of Longfellow as one of my first passions, and I have never ceased to delight in him; but some of the very newest and youngest of our poets have given me thrills of happiness, for which life has become lastingly sweeter. If I speak of a poem of Stoddard's, a sonnet of Aldrich's, a ballad of Stedman's, it is to offer partial payment on a sum in which I must always remain richly their debtor.

Long after I had thought never to read it — in fact when I was *nel mezzo del cammin di nostra vita* — I read Milton's Paradise Lost, and found in it a splendor and majestic beauty that justified to me the fame it wears, and eclipsed the worth of those lesser poems which I had stupidly and ignorantly accounted his worthiest. In fact it was one of the literary passions of the time I speak of, and it shared my devotion for the novels of Tourguenief and (shall I own it?) the romances of Cherbuliez. After all, it is best to be honest, and if it is not best, it is at least easiest; it involves the fewest embarrassing consequences; and if I confess the spell that the Revenge of Joseph Noirel cast upon me for a time, perhaps I shall be able to whisper the reader behind my hand that I have never yet read the Æneid of Virgil; the Georgics, yes; but the Æneid, no. Some time, however, I expect to read it and to like it immensely. That is often the case with things that I have held aloof from indefinitely.

One fact of my experience which the reader may find interesting is that when I am writing steadily I have little relish for reading. I fancy that reading is not merely a pastime when it is apparently the merest pastime, but that a certain measure of mind-stuff is used up in it, and that if you are using up all the mind-stuff you have, much or little, in some other way, you do not read because you have not the mind-stuff for it. At any rate it is in this sort only that I can account for my failure to read a great deal during four years of the amplest quiet that I spent in the country at Belmont, whither we removed from Cambridge. I had promised myself that in this quiet, now that I had given up reviewing, and wrote little or nothing in the magazine but my stories, I should again read purely for the pleasure of it, as I had in the early days before the critical purpose had qualified it with a bitter alloy. But I found that not being forced to read a number of books each month, so that I might write about them, I did not read at all, comparatively speaking. To be sure I dawdled over a great many books that I

had read before, and a number of memoirs and biog-
raphies, but I had no intense pleasure from reading in
that time, and have no passions to record of it. It
may have been a period when no new thing happened
in literature freshly to stir one's interest; I only state
the fact concerning myself, and suggest the most plau-
sible theory I can think of.

I wish also to note another incident, which may or
may not have its psychological value. An important
event of these years was a long sickness which kept
me helpless some seven or eight weeks, when I was
forced to read in order to pass the intolerable time.
But in this misery I found that I could not read anything of a dramatic cast, whether in the form of plays
or of novels. The mere sight of the printed page,
broken up in dialogue, was anguish. Yet it was not
the excitement of the fiction that I dreaded, for I con-
sumed great numbers of narratives of travel, and was
not in the least troubled by hairbreadth escapes, or
shipwrecks, or perils from wild beasts or deadly ser-
pents; it was the dramatic effect contrived by the
playwright or novelist, and worked up to in the speech
of his characters that I could not bear. I found a like
impossible stress from the Sunday newspaper which a
mistaken friend sent in to me, and which with its

scare-headings, and artfully-wrought sensations, had the effect of fiction, as in fact it largely was.

At the end of four years we went abroad again, and travel took away the appetite for reading as completely as writing did. I recall nothing read in that year in Europe which moved me, and I think I read very little, except the local histories of the Tuscan cities which I afterward wrote of.

XXXIV

VALERA, VALDÉS, GALDÓS, VERGA, ZOLA,
TROLLOPE, HARDY.

In fact, it was not till I returned, and took up life again in Boston, in the old atmosphere of work, that I turned once more to books. Even then I had to wait for the time when I undertook a critical department in one of the magazines, before I felt the rise of the old enthusiasm for an author. That is to say, I had to begin reading for business again before I began reading for pleasure. The first great pleasure which I had upon these terms was in the book of a contemporary Spanish author, the Pepita Ximenez of Juan Valera. It is not a book that I could commend without reserve to the reading of young people, but after frankly confessing this I must say that it is, even by our standard, a far more blameless book than half the fiction I know, and beside most stage plays it is exemplary. What took me in it was the charm of an

exquisite art in a direction where I had never thought
to turn again, and a fresh and joyous sympathy with
human nature in an absolutely novel phase. It is a
daring story for a Catholic to have written, but one
gets used to such daring in the modern Spanish
authors.

The next Spanish book that fell into my hands was
a still more striking instance of their boldness in dealing with the visible church. This was the Marta y
María of Armando Palacio Valdés, a novelist who delights me beyond words by his friendly and abundant
humor, his feeling for character, and his subtle insight. I like every one of his books that I have read,
and I believe that I have read nearly every one that he
has written. As I mention Riverito, Maximina, Un
Idilio de un Inferno, La Hermana de San Sulpizio, El
Cuarto Poder, Espuma, the mere names conjure up the
scenes and events that have moved me to tears and
laughter, and filled me with a vivid sense of the life
portrayed in them. I think the Marta y María one of
the most truthful and profound fictions I have read,
and Maximina one of the most pathetic, and La Hermana de San Sulpizio one of the most amusing. For-
tunately, these books of Valdés's have nearly all been
translated, and the reader may test the matter in

English, though it necessarily halts somewhat behind the Spanish.

I do not know whether the Spaniards themselves rank Valdés with Galdós or not, and I have no wish to decide upon their relative merits. They are both present passions of mine, and I may say of the Doña Perfecta of Galdós that no book, if I except those of the greatest Russians, has given me a keener and deeper impression; it is infinitely pathetic, and is full of humor, which if more caustic than that of Valdés is not less delicious. But I like all the books of Galdós that I have read, and though he seems to have worked more tardily out of his romanticism than Valdés, since he has worked finally into such realism as that of Leon Roch, his greatness leaves nothing to be desired.

I have read one of the books of Emilia Pardo-Bazan, called Morriña, which must rank her with the great realists of her country and age; she, too, has that humor of her race, which brings us nearer the Spanish than any other non-Anglo-Saxon people.

A contemporary Italian, whom I like hardly less than these noble Spaniards, is Giovanni Verga, who wrote I Malavoglia, or, as we call it in English, The House by the Medlar Tree: a story of infinite beauty,

tenderness and truth.   As I have said before, I think
with Zola that Giacometti, the Italian author of La
Morte Civile, has written almost the greatest play, all
round, of modern times.

But what shall I say of Zola himself, and my admiration of his epic greatness?   About his material there
is no disputing among people of our Puritanic tradition.   It is simply abhorrent, but when you have once
granted him his material for his own use, it is idle and
foolish to deny his power.   Every literary theory of
mine was contrary to him when I took up L'Assom-
moir, though unconsciously I had always been as much
of a realist as I could, but the book possessed me with
the same fascination that I felt the other day in reading his L'Argent.   The critics know now that Zola is
not the realist he used to fancy himself, and he is full
of the best qualities of the romanticism he has hated
so much; but for what he is, there is but one novelist
of our time, or of any, that outmasters him, and that
is Tolstoy.   For my own part, I think that the books
of Zola are not immoral, but they are indecent through
the facts that they nakedly represent; they are infinitely more moral than the books of any other French
novelist.   This may not be saying a great deal, but it
is saying the truth, and I do not mind owning that he

has been one of my great literary passions, almost as great as Flaubert, and greater than Daudet or Maupassant, though I have profoundly appreciated the exquisite artistry of both these. No French writer, however, has moved me so much as the Spanish, for the French are wanting in the humor which endears these, and is the quintessence of their charm.

You cannot be at perfect ease with a friend who does not joke, and I suppose this is what deprived me of a final satisfaction in the company of Anthony Trollope, who jokes heavily or not at all, and whom I should otherwise make bold to declare the greatest of English novelists; as it is, I must put before him Jane Austen, whose books, late in life, have been a youthful rapture with me. Even without much humor Trollope's books have been a vast pleasure to me through their simple truthfulness. Perhaps if they were more humorous they would not be so true to the British life and character present in them in the whole length and breadth of its expansive commonplaceness. It is their serious fidelity which gives them a value unique in literature, and which if it were carefully analyzed would afford a principle of the same quality in an author who was undoubtedly one of the finest of artists as well as the most Philistine of men.

I came rather late, but I came with all the ardor of what seems my perennial literary youth, to the love of Thomas Hardy, whom I first knew in his story A Pair of Blue Eyes. As usual, after I had read this book and felt the new charm in it, I wished to read the books of no other author, and to read his books over and over. I could not get enough of them, though with a characteristic perversity or fatality I have not yet read his Tess. I love even the faults of Hardy; I will let him play me any trick he chooses (and he is not above playing tricks, when he seems to get tired of his story or perplexed with it), if only he will go on making his peasants talk, and his rather uncertain ladies get in and out of love, and serve themselves of every chance that fortune offers them of having their own way. We shrink from the unmorality of the Latin races, but Hardy has divined in the heart of our own race a lingering heathenism, which, if not Greek, has certainly been no more baptized than the neo-hellenism of the Parisians. His heroines especially exemplify it, and I should be safe in saying that his Ethelbertas, his Eustacias, his Elfridas, his Bathshebas, his Fancies, are wholly pagan. I should not dare to ask how much of their charm came from that fact; and the author does not fail to show you how much harm, so that it is not on my conscience. His people live very close to the heart of nature, and no one, unless it is Tourguenief, gives you a richer and sweeter sense of her unity with human nature. Hardy is a great poet as well as a great humorist, and if he were not a great artist also his humor would be enough to make him dear to me.

XXXV.

TOLSTOY.

I COME now, though not quite in the order of time, to the noblest of all these enthusiasms, namely, my devotion for the writings of Lyof Tolstoy. I should wish to speak of him with his own incomparable truth, yet I do not know how to give a notion of his influence without the effect of exaggeration. As much as one merely human being can help another I believe that he has helped me; he has not influenced me in æsthetics only, but in ethics, too, so that I can never again see life in the way I saw it before I knew him. Tolstoy awakens in his reader the will to be a man; not effectively, not spectacularly, but simply, really. He leads you back to the only true ideal, away from that false standard of the gentleman, to the Man who sought not to be distinguished from other men, but identified with them, to that Presence in which the finest gentleman shows his alloy of vanity, and the greatest genius shrinks to the measure of his miserable egotism. I learned from Tolstoy to try character and motive by no other test, and though I am perpetually false to that sublime ideal myself, still the ideal remains with me, to make me ashamed that I am not true to it. Tolstoy gave me heart to hope that the world may yet be made over in the image of Him who died for it, when all Cæsar's things shall be finally rendered unto Cæsar, and men shall come into their own, into the right to labor and the right to enjoy the fruits of their labor, each one master of himself and servant to every other. He taught me to see life not as a chase of a forever impossible personal happiness, but as a field for endeavor toward the happiness of the whole human family; and I can never lose this vision, however I close my eyes, and strive to see my own interest as the highest good. He gave me new criterions, new principles, which, after all, were those that are taught us in our earliest childhood, before we have come to the evil wisdom of the world. As I read his different ethical books, What to Do, My Confession, and My Religion, I recognized their truth with a rapture such as I have known in no other reading, and I rendered them my allegiance, heart and soul, with whatever sickness of the one and despair of the other. They have it yet, and I believe they will have it while I live. It is with inexpressible astonishment that I hear them attainted of pessimism, as if the teaching of a man whose ideal was simple goodness must mean the prevalence of evil. The way he showed me seemed indeed impossible to my will, but to my conscience it was and is the only possible way. If there is any point on which he has not convinced my reason it is that of our ability to walk this narrow way alone. Even there he is logical, but as Zola subtly distinguishes in speaking of Tolstoy's essay on Money, he is not reasonable. Solitude enfeebles and palsies, and it is as comrades and brothers that men must save the world from itself, rather than themselves from the world. It was so the earliest Christians, who had all things common, understood the life of Christ, and I believe that the latest will understand it so.

I have spoken first of the ethical works of Tolstoy, because they are of the first importance to me, but I think that his æsthetical works are as perfect. To my thinking they transcend in truth, which is the highest beauty, all other works of fiction that have been written, and I believe that they do this because they obey the law of the author's own life. His conscience is one ethically and one æsthetically; with his will to be true to himself he cannot be false to his knowledge of others. I thought the last word in literary art had been said to me by the novels of Tourguenief, but it seemed like the first, merely, when I began to acquaint myself with the simpler method of Tolstoy. I came to it by accident, and without any manner of preoccupation in The Cossacks, one of his early books, which had been on my shelves unread for five or six years. I did not know even Tolstoy's name when I opened it, and it was with a kind of amaze that I read it, and felt word by word, and line by line, the truth of a new art in it.

I do not know how it is that the great Russians have the secret of simplicity. Some say it is because they have not a long literary past and are not conventionalized by the usage of many generations of other writers, but this will hardly account for the brotherly directness of their dealing with human nature; the absence of experience elsewhere characterizes the artist with crudeness, and simplicity is the last effect of knowledge. Tolstoy is, of course, the first of them in this supreme grace. He has not only Tourguenief's transparency of style, unclouded by any mist of the personality which we mistakenly value in style, and

which ought no more to be there than the artist's personality should be in a portrait; but he has a method
which not only seems without artifice, but is so.   I
can get at the manner of most writers, and tell what
it is, but I should be baffled to tell what Tolstoy's
manner is; perhaps he has no manner.   This appears
to me true of his novels, which, with their vast variety
of character and incident, are alike in their single endeavor to get the persons living before you, both in
their action and in the peculiarly dramatic interpreta-
tion of their emotion and cogitation.   There are plenty
of novelists to tell you that their characters felt and
thought so and so, but you have to take it on trust;
Tolstoy alone makes you know how and why it was so
with them and not otherwise.   If there is anything in
him which can be copied or burlesqued it is this ability of his to show men inwardly as well as outwardly;
it is the only trait of his which I can put my hand on.

After the Cossacks I read Anna Karenina with a
deepening sense of the author's unrivaled greatness. I
thought that I saw through his eyes a human affair of
that most sorrowful sort as it must appear to the Infinite Compassion; the book is a sort of revelation of
human nature in circumstances that have been so perpetually lied about that we have almost lost the faculty

of perceiving the truth concerning an illicit love. When you have once read Anna Karenina you know how fatally miserable and essentially unhappy such a love must be. But the character of Karenin himself is quite as important as the intrigue of Anna and Vronsky. It is wonderful how such a man, cold, Philistine and even mean in certain ways, towers into a sublimity unknown (to me, at least,) in fiction when he forgives, and yet knows that he cannot forgive with dignity. There is something crucial, and something triumphant, not beyond the power, but hitherto beyond the imagination of men in this effect, which is not solicited, not forced, not in the least romantic, but comes naturally, almost inevitably from the make of man.

The vast prospects, the far-reaching perspectives of War and Peace made it as great a surprise for me in the historical novel as Anna Karenina had been in the study of contemporary life; and its people and interests did not seem more remote, since they are of a civilization always as strange and of a humanity always as known.

I read some shorter stories of Tolstoy's before I came to this greatest work of his: I read Scenes of the Siege of Sebastopol, which is so much of the same quality as War and Peace; and I read Policoushka and most of his short stories with a sense of my unity with their people such as I had never felt with the people of other fiction.

His didactic stories, like all stories of the sort, dwindle into allegories; perhaps they do their work the better for this, with the simple intelligences they address; but I think that where Tolstoy becomes impatient of his office of artist, and prefers to be directly a teacher, he robs himself of more than half his strength with those he can move only through the realization of themselves in others. The simple pathos, and the apparent indirectness of such a tale as that of Policoushka, the peasant conscript, is of vastly more value to the world at large than all his parables; and The Death of Ivan Ilyitch, the Philistine worldling, will turn the hearts of many more from the love of the world than such pale fables of the early Christian life as Work while ye have the Light. A man's gifts are not given him for nothing, and the man who has the great gift of dramatic fiction has no right to cast it away or to let it rust out in disuse.

Terrible as the Kreutzer Sonata was, it had a moral effect dramatically which it lost altogether when the author descended to exegesis, and applied to marriage the lesson of one evil marriage. In fine, Tolstoy is certainly not to be held up as infallible. He is very distinctly fallible, but I think his life is not less instructive because in certain things it seems a failure. There was but one life ever lived upon the earth which was without failure, and that was Christ's, whose erring and stumbling follower Tolstoy is. There is no other example, no other ideal, and the chief use of Tolstoy is to enforce this fact in our age, after nineteen centuries of hopeless endeavor to substitute ceremony for character, and the creed for the life. I recognize the truth of this without pretending to have been changed in anything but my point of view of it. What I feel sure is that I can never look at life in the mean and sordid way that I did before I read Tolstoy.

Artistically, he has shown me a greatness that he can never teach me. I am long past the age when I could wish to form myself upon another writer, and I do not think I could now insensibly take on the likeness of another; but his work has been a revelation and a delight to me, such as I am sure I can never know again. I do not believe that in the whole course of my reading, and not even in the early moment of my literary enthusiasms, I have known such utter satisfaction in any writer, and this supreme joy has come to me at a time of life when new friendships, not to say new passions, are rare and reluctant. It is as if the best wine at this high feast where I have sat so long had been kept for the last, and I need not deny a miracle in it in order to attest my skill in judging vintages. In fact, I prefer to believe that my life has been full of miracles, and that the good has always come to me at the right time, so that I could profit most by it. I believe if I had not turned the corner of my fiftieth year, when I first knew Tolstoy, I should not have been able to know him as fully as I did. He has been to me that final consciousness, which he speaks of so wisely in his essay on Life. I came in it to the knowledge of myself in ways I had not dreamt of before, and began at least to discern my relations to the race, without which we are each nothing. The supreme art in literature had its highest effect in making me set art forever below humanity, and it is with the wish to offer the greatest homage to his heart and mind, which any man can pay another, that I close this record with the name of Lyof Tolstoy.

INDEX.

———◆———

THE END.